THE HILL

St. Louis's Italian American Neighborhood

Reedy Press
PO Box 5131
St. Louis, MO 63139
www.reedypress.com

Library of Congress Control Number: 2020938255

ISBN: 9781681062884

Design: Jill Halpin and Eric Marquard
Layout: Linda Eckels

All images courtesy of The Hill Neighborhood Center unless otherwise noted.
Cover images: Top image–Cory Weaver; Volpi, Virgin Mary–Jill Halpin, Piazzi, Milo's–Barbara Northcott

Printed in the United States
20 21 22 23 24   5 4 3 2 1

Credit: Barbara Northcott

DEDICATION

This book is dedicated to the people of The Hill.

THE HILL

St. Louis's Italian American Neighborhood

LynnMarie Alexander
Foreword by Joseph DeGregorio

Credit: Barbara Northcott

TABLE OF CONTENTS

FOREWORD

In 2005, after retiring from 30 years of federal service in national security disciplines, I felt it was time for a change—time to have some fun. My dad, Roland DeGregorio, had a suggestion for me: *Son, you have a degree in broadcast journalism from MU plus a master's degree. If you're willing to do some research, I know you can do tours of The Hill.* Dad was winding down from some 25 years of providing Hill tours after retiring as the neighborhood's main mailman for 25 years. But I wasn't so sure about his advice: *Dad, I don't have your knowledge, and I haven't had the experiences of the people who've lived there all their lives.* Although I had visited many, many times, I hadn't lived there since 1972.

But dad wasn't hearing excuses: *You'll figure it out, and I'll give you all my archives to help get you started.* It was tough—not the researching part or actually conducting tours, but seeing the look on the faces of many residents who were thinking (and sometimes saying out loud), *You don't know as much as your father, and you'll probably make some of the stuff up just like he did!* It took around five years before I started getting approving nods and comments like *I heard you're doing a great job—keep it up!* It was only then that this prodigal son of The Hill felt his efforts had earned the "respecto" not only of the then-dwindling first generation of Italian Americans, but, just as importantly, of the residents from my generation—the baby boomers, most especially Msgr. Bommarito, longtime pastor of St. Ambrose.

In my many business and vacation travels I have visited most of the major Little Italies in the US. Most appeared to be mere shells of what they were 100 years ago. For this reason I can say that The Hill is the last real Italian *neighborhood* in the country!

As you embark on your personal tour of this visually pleasing and historically enlightening quilt, beautifully stitched together by LynnMarie Alexander, you'll find the elements you expect, such as a description of The Hill from its humble beginnings to the present day, along with profiles of Yogi Berra and Joe Garagiola. But to provide a little something for everyone, we've also included things like the almost-forgotten details of two divas from the past who have strong Hill connections, descriptions of the local musicals produced here in the '60s and '70s. And perhaps for the first time in a book format, we have included reminiscences of Hill residents who grew up during and immediately after World War II—mainly second-generation Italian Americans who have proudly carried the baton of our Italian heritage. They are old enough to remember many of the original immigrants who made The Hill the unique place it is, yet they have also witnessed its repopulation with younger people and families.

We boomers are now slowly passing our neighborhood's legacy to future generations of Italian Americans and, yes, even to those with no Italian lineage who are moving in. Along with the new faces there are many new and remodeled homes—even here, the winds of change are always in the air. Still, the character that defines The Hill is safe in the hands of a committed base of residents led by our alderman, Joe Vollmer, and *siempre* St. Ambrose Church—the real anchor of our community. As a home for those who celebrate its traditions and also those who want to help write the next chapter of its history, the future of The Hill is bright.

—Joseph DeGregorio

INTRODUCTION

This book is a celebration of the people of The Hill, past and present. Whether they claim five generations of familial legacy or have recently moved to The Hill, they know they are in a special neighborhood. While The Hill's reputation for tidiness and safety is rooted in generations of habit, those newly moved to the area embrace and participate in our community. They enjoy the Italian atmosphere in the form of a bounty of Italian eateries; a spiritual community centered around Saint Ambrose Church, Saint Ambrose Grade School, and the Sacred Heart Villa daycare and nursery; events such as the Italian Heritage Parade; and pastimes like bocce leagues, soccer, and even opera. They value being in a passionate community that is equally enthusiastic about sports, music, and simple celebrations with friends and family. Those with firm roots in Italy appreciate the opportunities the United States provided their forefathers, who made good by being successful entrepreneurs or professionals and who did not waiver when it was time to defend their adopted country or support the neighborhood in which they were born.

The information presented here, housed in The Hill 2000 Neighborhood Association archives, was gleaned from original documents including publications such as *The Hill 2000 Newsletter*, the *Crusader Clarion,* and various studies and publications about The Hill. Photographs and original documents donated by the community serve to infuse The Hill's history with rich detail.

This historical narrative follows the treatises by Gary Mormino and Eleanore Berra-Marfisi, which use first-person accounts to keep The Hill's past alive. Cavaliere Films' documentary on The Hill empowered Hill residents to tell their stories in their own voice.

I ask for leniency from my Hill neighbors as they will surely think I have not covered the whole story. And they would be correct. Even with the story told here and by the amazing sources mentioned above, there is always more to learn.

Longevity is The Hill's secret. Families stay, and businesses grow old yet still grow. Our institutional memory is strong, and we are blessed. That's *amore*!

Credit: Cory Weaver

ACKNOWLEDGMENTS

 This book was built on the information housed in The Hill Neighborhood Center. The riches of the Center's archives came from donations by the community, including timeless photos, original documents, neighborhood newsletters, Hill memorabilia, and other pieces of history that bring The Hill's past to life. Center volunteers Bob Miriani, Mary Ann Pirone, and Don Torretti offer a day of service each week. Newer volunteer Bob Traina has taken on the Herculean task of organizing five years of photos from the *Crusader Clarion*. The Hill House Tour committees of 2018 and 2019 poured hours of time and effort into ensuring that the events were a spectacular success, raising thousands of dollars in support of the Center. I am grateful to the other volunteers, too numerous to mention, who pitched in with their hard work, sanity, and humor.

The Hill business community and benefactors contribute money and time to endeavors that keep The Hill new and vibrant. The Hill 2000 Neighborhood Association manages The Hill Neighborhood Center and serves the community, aiming to maintain its history, health, and solidarity. St. Ambrose Catholic Church binds the partnership as spiritual center and bastion of stability. I am grateful for their investment in our long-lived community.

I am grateful to Joe DeGregorio for his generous support of The Hill Neighborhood Center through donations of funds, time, and a collection of valuable memorabilia. He graciously entrusted me with this project. Thank you to Rio Vitale for proposing the idea and for adding your memories of a beloved community leader. George Venegoni's recollections and his feedback proved invaluable. Thank you, George, for corralling Kathy Bagby, Joyce Clyne, and Tony Zona's memories. Thank you, Joe, for encouraging Paul DeGregorio and Dea Hoover to participate. Each author added precious depth and authenticity. The book has a voice because of them.

My deepest gratitude goes to Reedy Press's Josh Stevens and Barbara Northcott, who walked this newbie author through a seemingly daunting task. I appreciate their expertise and grace.

My husband, Danny Alexander, and my mother, Ann (Puricelli) Sanders, indulged my angst in its many forms throughout this project. I appreciate their support. Even though they are not ones to say I told you so, I really did enjoy writing this book about a place and people who I think are pretty darn awesome!

And finally to those reading this book, the following pages merely mention the highlights of Hill history. There is more to explore. To those who participate, thank you; to those who are curious, keep asking; to those who want to be involved, welcome. To the rest, enjoy. *Grazie.*

EARLY HISTORY AND ESTABLISHMENT

PLOTTING THE LAND

The Mississippian culture thrived along the Mississippi Valley roughly between 700 and 1200 CE, disappearing completely before the first Europeans arrived. The population of its urban center, Cahokia (in present-day Illinois), reached nearly 15,000 at its zenith, making it the largest indigenous city-state north of the Rio Grande. Cahokia holds the remains of the Mississippian's characteristic mound dwellings. Archeologists speculate that the mounds represented a stratified society of elites and laborers, though the economy operated on a barter system rather than pay for labor. They were the first organized settlers at the confluence of the Mississippi and Missouri Rivers, and their mysterious disappearance left many questions regarding their everyday life.

Charles Gratiot's League Square grant from the Spanish territorial government in 1798 encompassed what was to become The Hill and neighboring communities to the west. Gratiot was born in Switzerland with familial roots in France. He was educated in England, moved to the United States to fight in the American Revolution and make his fortune, and learned Spanish along the way. He settled in St. Louis, where he built his "city house" on Chestnut and Second Streets.

He acted as official translator during the 1804 Louisiana Purchase ceremony and for conversations between Meriwether Lewis and the Spanish governor Delassus. He married Victoire Chouteau, daughter of Pierre Chouteau, who was a member of a prominent early St. Louis family. His daughters married into the Laclede, De Mun, and Labadie families, which built hugely successful businesses and are among St. Louis's founding families.

Gratiot's land grant encompassed roughly a three-square-mile patch. He named the north–south thoroughfare that formed the eastern boundary of the land "King's Highway" in an unsuccessful attempt to attract support from the Spanish government in maintaining this 40-foot-wide road.

Gratiot's "country home" was perched on top of an incline at present-day Macklind and Pattison overlooking the River des Peres next to the few buildings that were built close to a nearby railroad stop. Disembarking passengers from the Missouri Pacific line at Howard Station in Cheltenham enjoyed the services of the Sulphur Springs Hotel and Gittins Hotel and Saloon.

The Gratiot family maintained possession of their League Square for three generations before dividing it into 12 east–west strips and selling these to landowners such as Mrs. Frances Sublette, Peter Lindell, Henry Shaw, and J. F. Cooper.

Prior to the Civil War, the Cooper tract just west of Kingshighway became the first site for a remote residential area, which was called Garden Place and was located five miles from the Mississippi riverfront. Newly discovered sulfur springs enticed city residents to visit the countryside for the therapeutic benefits of the springs.

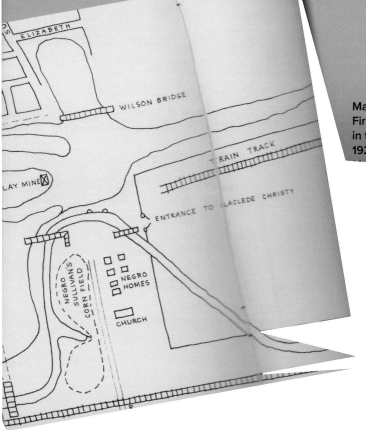

Map of the Laclede Christy Fire Clay Company site in the Fairmount district, 1923, original map by

CLAY MINES

The Cheltenham district's local clay, known as "fireclay," developed millions of years ago through unique organic processes that left the material especially tolerant of high heat and therefore desirable for steam train engines and long-term projects such as underground municipal pipes. It has a rich, deep color that exaggerates the common term "brick red." Other types of clay found in the area range widely in hue from cinnamon to browns to yellows to creams. A pattern of bricks of all these types in one building or in a row of structures where each hue differs from the next presents a visual kaleidoscope. As foundries advanced in technology, they glazed individual bricks with beautiful bronze, emerald green, cobalt blue, and pearl white surfaces that festively decorate facades, porches, and columns. What seemed common became beautiful.

The first clay processing plant in Gratiot's League Square was built by English Quakers in 1844. After the Pacific Railroad added a stop in Cheltenham in 1852, supplies and labor streamed into the area. The Evens & Howard Fire Brick Company constructed a factory in 1855, followed by the Laclede Christy Fire Clay Company in 1857. The events of 1849 presented a major opportunity for the St. Louis brick industry. A Mississippi riverboat moored at the central commercial landing caught fire. Over a 24-hour period, the fire consumed 418 wooden structures over a 15-block area, making it still the single worst disaster in St. Louis history. The city government mandated that new buildings be constructed of brick in order to avoid a similar catastrophe in the future.

Circumstances, resources, and opportunity combined to make St. Louis the premier brick maker for the United States for the next several decades. Cheltenham and the former Gratiot League Square were at the center of the industry.

Rapid industrial development followed the Civil War. The growing railroad companies transported materials to thriving cities and newly opened territories in the south and west. Clay and coal miners fed brick works and foundries, and they manufactured items necessary to make industry flourish.

The mining legacy extended into the 20th century. There are buildings and backyards on The Hill that connected to the few remaining intact tunnels, though they have been carefully locked, covered, or even cemented shut. Residents of The Hill used their tunneling skills to create an underground network to make and move wine and moonshine during the Prohibition era. Seniors today recall their own experiences as children playing around the closed mines and shaft entrances. They also remember the rare occasions when they or a friend fell through a weak spot on a shaft roof. Going home was worse than the accident since they had to admit that they disobeyed their parents' warnings to stay clear.

The last working shaft closed in the early 1940s, and the tunnel entrances were sealed. The clay and soft coal veins were depleted, and the post-World War II global economy found more efficient ways to produce replacements for bricks.

While they were in operation, however, the mines changed the nature of labor in the Cheltenham district. Freed African Americans as well as immigrants from Germany, Ireland, and Italy worked in overlapping waves in the mines and factories.

IMMIGRATION

In 1853, French Utopian Etienne Cabet and his 200 followers (called "Icarians") settled on 28 acres in northwest Cheltenham in an area previously occupied by the Sulphur Springs Resort. Cabet and his communal visionaries built small cabins, shared labor, and pursued the humanities via theater, music, poetry, and literature. Their experiment lasted 11 years before succumbing to the challenges of disease brought by pollution and insects infesting the River des Peres, internal dissention after Cabet died, and financial mismanagement.

Where jobs were plentiful, laborers followed. Initially the area neighboring Cheltenham was known as the Fairmount district (The Hill today). It was bounded by New Manchester, Kingshighway, Old Manchester (Southwest Ave.), and Hampton, and it hosted diverse ethnic groups including African Americans, Irish, Germans, and Italians.

As their respective numbers grew in Cheltenham, the populace segregated along parish lines. St. James the Greater Catholic Church (1861) centered the mostly Irish community to the west of Hampton. Germans settled slightly southwest in the St. Aloysius Gonzaga Church parish (1892), which was in place before the increased Italian presence and acted as a temporary missionary church for the Italian community. The Italians settled within the Fairmount district, eventually building **St. Ambrose Church (1903)**.

The Pattison Avenue Baptist Church (1897) stood on the land near the Gratiot country home overlooking the River des Peres, which was used in the early years as a full-immersion baptismal fount. The African American congregants continued to worship at the church until the building was demolished to clear the path for Highway 44. The congregation moved to a new church still named the Pattison Avenue Baptist Church but now located on DeBaliviere Avenue near Delmar Boulevard in St. Louis.

From 1889 to 1910, the **Bethlehem German Evangelical Church** stood at the corner of Shaw and Hereford. As the German population moved to the south and west of The Hill, their church followed to Southwest Avenue. In 1928, it merged with the Messiah Evangelical Church, forming the Mount Tabor Church on Arsenal. The Catholic Church purchased the original building at Shaw and Hereford in 1919.

The Italian Evangelical Church was founded in 1921 by Italian Protestant minister Peter Ottolini, and it moved to its present location on Botanical in 1929. In 1994, the church became home to the **Bansuk Korean Baptist Church**. The church building was popularly known as the "Rabbit Church" (or in an Italian dialect as the "cunnelie" church) because of its distinct dual spire design, suggesting rabbit ears.

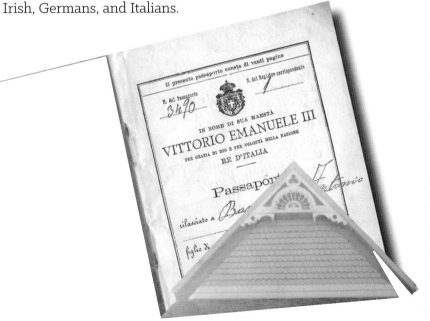

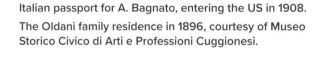

Italian passport for A. Bagnato, entering the US in 1908.

The Oldani family residence in 1896, courtesy of Museo Storico Civico di Arti e Professioni Cuggionesi.

Credit: Jill Halpin

Credit: Jill Halpin

Volpi's and Gioia's celebrated their 100th birthdays in 2007 and 2018, respectively, while the youngster, Missouri Baking Company, looks forward to its centennial in 2024.

SETTLEMENT

Between the rule of the Romans and the 20th century, the peninsular landmass now known as Italy and the nearby islands were a group of nation-states, each with their own regional customs, political organization, labor practices, and cuisines. Italy became today's modern democratic nation in four historic warring stages dating from 1848 to 1918.

Immigrants to The Hill came from two general regional areas: Lombardy in the north and Sicily in the south. Both groups sought relief from oppressive landlords who treated their tenants like serfs. There were few jobs other than working the animals, toiling in the fields, or fishing the sea. Taxes on the products of their labor frequently left the villagers starving. The promise of America enticed young and old alike to take a chance in a new foreign country. The first to come from his village must have been brave to walk or take a carriage to the port in Le Havre, Calais, Genoa, or Palermo. Immigrants endured a crowded ship replete with thieves and illness. Once in America, they had to pass through immigration, hoping their papers were in order and that they were not ill. Either could be cause for rejection and a return home. Harried and often unsympathetic immigration officers may have "heard with an accent" or had poor penmanship, resulting in misspelled names. Anyone doing family research knows the frustration of tracking a relative with a changed name.

Once the immigrants arrived in New York or New Orleans, they needed to adjust quickly. They did not know the language and must have been baffled by the customs and activity of a large city. They made their way to the train stations and boarded for the days-long journey to their destination. Upon arrival, they were shocked to find streets that were paved not with gold, but with a lot of mud.

While conditions were harsh, opportunity always beckoned. If a family worked hard and used their money wisely, they could become as wealthy as the landowner they escaped. They could buy more than one house and use the second or third as an investment, something unheard of in the old country. While some families on The Hill started businesses in St. Louis, others brought their trade and expertise with them. Several families created construction companies or supplied the building trades and have done very well. Other families invested in specialty food items such as salamis or pizza, while others built long-standing restaurants, delis, and groceries. A dozen or more businesses built by Hill families are over 50 years old, while some have even passed their 100-year anniversary.

Top: St. Ambrose first communion

Left: Nick Mazzola and friends

Right: Children attending Sacred Heart Villa anticipate picnic day.

NORTHERN AND SOUTHERN ITALIANS

Cultural differences within the Italian American community could have cracked its foundation. The initial Italian immigrants came from villages outside of Milan, in the Lombardy region in the north of Italy. They spoke in a Lombard dialect incomprehensible to Italians who lived further south. A smaller percentage came from Genoa, the Piedmont region, and from Sicily.

The lower Alpine Lombard diet consisted of dairy, rice, grains, beef, pork, and a tendency toward root vegetables. Their staple dishes include now-popular risotto, polenta, ravioli, cheeses, and cured meats (salami).

They came to St. Louis and settled in the Fairmount district to work as miners and clay masons. Men from villages outside of Milan came, sending for their families or brides-to-be after they earned enough to build a house. They became successful entrepreneurs, starting businesses such as groceries, general stores, taverns, and eventually restaurants.

They built St. Ambrose Church and School, but the Big Club Hall was their neighborhood focal point. It was the place to find work and lodging, get help with citizenship papers, become involved in local activities, establish relationships within the community, or purchase necessities at the co-op. It was also

the place for wedding receptions, live music in the Blue Room, and New Year's Eve parties. The Riggio Realty Company (and bank), now Shaw Coffee, played a significant role in legal matters, housing, and overseas transportation for newly arrived immigrants.

While community activities flourished on The Hill, most Italians from Sicily settled near the Mississippi in the downtown area. They were anchored by Our Lady Help of Christians Catholic Church, and they spoke in the Sicilian dialect. They worked in the produce industry supplying the St. Louis area with fruits, vegetables, and flowers. By the 1930s, the "downtown Italians" felt pressure on their community from population shift and the effects it had on their own businesses. By the 1950s, the downtown Italian community had disintegrated, and families moved to the northern part of St. Louis or to The Hill.

Lombards and Sicilians initially had difficulty coexisting. It took a generation to shed biases and for the community to come together. Language and culture proved to be the highest hurdles. When speaking in dialect, Lombards and Sicilians simply could not understand each other. Culinary practices also magnified the north–south cultural differences. The Mediterranean, semitropical Sicilian diet was based on the sea. Proteins included fish and a bit of pork, served with olive oil, vine vegetables and fruits, bread, and pasta. Sicilians were early adopters of tomato and eggplant.

The Hill residents made the best of the situation. Immigrants from Sicily established their own organizations such as the Unione Sicilanna Principeda Piedmonte and the Palma Augusta. The latter became the reception hall counterpart to the Big Club Hall, where residents and nonresidents attended wedding receptions, parties, political rallies, and community meetings. The Palma Augusta closed decades ago, though the Sicilians

The drum corps marches in a Corpus Christi parade.

maintain their roots through organizations such as UNICO and the Sicilian Club.

At one time, families strongly opposed marriage between a Lombard and a Sicilian. They would rather their child marry an "Amerigani" or non-Italian if they couldn't find "one of their own." The Hill community no longer gives credence to the old stereotypes. All children speak English, and food evolved to suit an American palate so that it hardly resembles recipes from the old country and does not carry the culturally significant weight it once did. The church served its purpose as the bedrock of the neighborhood by being a necessary place where all are equal and welcome. Marriages between Italians of different regions are common and without stigma. Social organizations such as the Italian Club welcome anyone of Italian heritage to join without discrimination. It even allows people who are not Italian but are fans of Italy to join as "amici."

Opposite page: During Mussolini's very early years, he invited young Italian men from The Hill to Italy to learn the Italian language.

PICTURE BRIDES AND MUTUAL AID SOCIETIES

The Fairmount district in 1890s St. Louis was no place for a good Italian young woman, much less to raise a family. The area was home to dirty coal and sticky clay mines, as well as factories that belched smoke and left soot on every flat surface. Streets were more mud than dirt, with few walkways on the side to allow pedestrians to avoid wagons, horses, and flying mud. Where absent planks left the street exposed, people clung to fencing on front yards to avoid street goop. Most houses were little more than rooms with beds where factory workers and miners slept in shifts. Food was purchased on the go from the tenant house owner, nearby grocer, or tavern. After a shift, men gathered at their favorite taverns and enjoyed the camaraderie and dialect of others from their family or village.

They came to America for more. Within 25 years, these intrepid men saved enough money to support a family, build a shotgun house, join a fraternal club, and create a Catholic church and school.

now that's *amore*

PICTURE BRIDES

Italian women in Italy and Italian men in America employed numerous methods of marital arrangements. When the men came in the 1890s, they planned to bring over their wives or wives-to-be as soon as they saved enough to buy a house. The American government issued visas designating a "married" or "betrothed" status for immigrant women. They rarely traveled alone, being instead accompanied by a father, uncle, brother, sister, grandmother, or aunt as chaperone. Once through immigration in New York or New Orleans, they traveled to St. Louis to meet their spouse or fiancé; in the latter case, a wedding usually followed within a week.

Some couples accepted arranged marriages brokered in the old country. They might have been very distant cousins, from the same village, or even meant to merge two family businesses. In this situation, when the intended bride and groom met for the first time, it was usually at the altar. As photography modernized, pictures of the intended were exchanged through the mail, though the marriage was rarely called off as a result.

MUTUAL AID SOCIETIES—SOCIAL

Mutual aid societies played crucial roles for newly arrived Italian Americans in St. Louis and on The Hill. Though many had specific missions, others resolved a plethora of issues facing immigrants every day. Contributing to The Hill's identity as a distinct Italian American community, mutual aid societies also created a feeling of belonging and protection. The parish priests joined long-established families by taking leadership responsibility for the well-being of the community as a whole. Residents responded by supporting Hill family businesses and the church. This symbiotic relationship has been strengthened by habit.

Fratellanza

Formed on November 12, 1866, the Fratellanza Society is the oldest continuing Italian American organization in the United States. It was founded to help newly arrived Italian immigrants adjust to their adopted home. As a fraternal and benevolent society for all Italian American men in St. Louis, it offered its members camaraderie and services such as employment help, housing location assistance, and even reduced cost for physician's services. Members paid monthly dues and were required to attend all Fratellanza meetings under penalty of fine if absent. Funeral services were

The first Fratellanza headquarters on Third Street, St. Louis

especially important since single men without family needed a proper burial. All members had to attend a brother's funeral or pay a five dollar fine. The weight of the fine has a basis in custom from the old country. Family members in Italy knew the Fratellanza ensured their loved one would receive a Catholic burial conducted by a priest and accompanied by dozens of friends from the funeral parlor to the gravesite, followed by the banquet that was usually the immediate family's responsibility. If the deceased's family ever traveled to St. Louis, they could find their loved one's gravestone.

The Fratellanza is still a men-only organization. Its legacy includes organizing the first Columbus Day Parade in St. Louis, a tradition that continues on The Hill today, while the organization's example of patriotism, charity, and brotherly love endures.

ONE HUNDRED AND FIFTIETH
ANNIVERSARY
OF THE
SOCIETA' UNIONE E FRATELLANZA ITALIANA
FRATELLANZA SOCIETY

One Hundred Fifty Years
150
S.U.F.I.
1866   2016
Cento Cinquanta Anni

SATURDAY NOVEMBER 12, 2016
SAINT LOUIS, MISSOURI

North Italian American Mercantile Company (and Cooperative) or Big Club Hall

The large square three-story building on the southwest corner of Shaw and Marconi once served as club, communal hangout, office space, (male) members-only tavern, reception hall, and entertainment venue. Founded in 1895, the space served as a gathering spot for newly arrived northern Italian immigrants to mingle with their well-established Lombard counterparts. Members visited the Big Club to find work, catch up on neighborhood news, play cards or bocce, or simply swap stories. They also purchased groceries and essential items at the cooperative in the building to the west or got a haircut at the barber near the east entrance. The Big Club Hall was known as "The Sport Center of The Hill" and during its latter years had a neon sign declaring it as such hanging in the tavern. It is now on display at Milo's Bocce Garden.

Big Club Hall housed offices on the second floor. By taking the back stairs, one could walk down the eerily narrow hallway to find small doors guarding even smaller offices with yellowed windows declaring the organization's name. Groups such as the Christopher Columbus Club, Liberty Legion of American Foundry, or Veterans of Foreign Wars conducted their affairs here.

In the early years of the Fairmount settlement, police services were scarce. The leadership of the Lombard fraternity enforced rules of conduct. There could be no street fights, especially ones drawing a crowd. If two men needed to work out a problem, they were expected to quietly take their dispute to the alley or pay a two dollar fine. As with other mutual aid societies the North Italian American Mercantile Company offered stock ownership in Big Club Hall's enterprises. Each person was limited as to how many stocks they could purchase so no one person had a voting advantage. Stocks were passed to an owner's son when the owner died. As a mutual aid society, it offered similar services in terms of employment and housing opportunities, death benefits, and funeral services.

Credit: Barbara Northcott

Big Club Hall wedding reception

MUTUAL AID SOCIETIES—CHURCH

Christian Mothers' Sodality (1904), also known as Madres Christiani, formed the first mutual aid society intended to support St. Ambrose Church and its pastor. **Our Lady of Mount Carmel** (1926) became the English-speaking branch of the sodality and is still active today. It raised funds for the improvement of the church and school (for example, the altar railing and the church organ were sponsored by the sister organizations). Today, they meet monthly for spiritual and enrichment programs, to assist with annual events such as the Easter egg hunt, to donate new purses filled with items useful to women in shelters, and to sell items at the annual Festa. Mt. Carmel Sodality members wear purple sashes and attend funerals of parish members to show support and assist as needed. The organization also facilitates the funerals of its members.

The St. Ambrose Men's Society formed in 1907 under Father Lucian Carotti's leadership. It initially included three hundred men who financed parish projects and supported the pastor and parish spiritually and financially. While this specific organization no longer exists, its legacy continues in the growth of newer mutual aid societies.

Clarion front page, January 1946

Mrs. Fassi, Maria Griffero, Maddalena Gualdoni, Ernesta Iovaldi, Erminia Ranzini, Maria Nazzoli, Tina Fuse, Giovanina Monti, Nunzia Russo, Virginia Pozzo, Maria Garascia, Giovanina Puricelli, and Joanne Arpiani. This photo, taken circa 1960, shows ladies from The Hill, accompanied by Tina Fuse and Joanne Arpiani, who appeared on the Charlotte Peters TV program to sing Italian songs. The wine was presented to Charlotte as a gift from the ladies.

The Crusader Club formed in 1935 for the "spiritual, material, and physical welfare of the young men and boys of the parish."

Initially it was divided into two subgroups determined by age, though it later merged into one. It is a mutual aid society, offering funeral benefits to its members and has become a legacy society in which most memberships are handed from father to son. Should no son be available, then another man is invited to take the open place. The Crusaders athletic teams excelled at soccer and baseball. Their lasting contribution to The Hill neighborhood was a monthly newsletter published during World War II that was exchanged between servicemen and neighborhood residents. Hill residents read not only about the men abroad but also about what was happening in their own community. Soldier, seaman, and airman alike looked forward to their monthly news from home. They also learned about the location of their brethren and

Holy Name Society Annual Safari
• by mary balmer •

JOE AIMONETTE AND MSGR. SAL POLIZZI

STEVE HILDERBRAND AND BOB HAWKINS

JACK STELZER AND HIS GRANDSON CHRIS WRIGHT

GENE CUCCHI AND MSGR. VINCE BOMMARITO

managed meetups while overseas. While the newsletter staff ended the publication in 1950, it still remains a detailed source of Hill history.

The Grail Club was a sisterhood organized by Father Adrian Dwyer in 1938. It became a counterpart to the Crusaders and assisted in Crusader projects. Women were encouraged to strengthen their faith but also to grow their mind and exercise their bodies. Young women learned about being professional and modern for themselves and for their children.

The St. Ambrose Alumni Association sprouted in response to the growing number of seventh-grade graduates. Sister Sylvester, St. Ambrose's principal, held the first alumni meeting in 1932. Its purpose was to permanently tie individuals to the community. It provided a way for graduates to stay in touch with each other, helped fortify a Catholic education for neighborhood students who attended public schools, and reminded members of their Catholic faith and obligations. The Alumni Association continues to meet for breakfast after a dedicated mass once a year, sitting together according to graduation year. St. Ambrose's eighth-graders serve the alumni, knowing they'll be included the next year. Though Joe Garagiola came home to The Hill many times a year, he tried to make every Alumni Breakfast and occasionally served as a guest speaker.

The Knights of Columbus is a fraternal organization whose members are Roman Catholic males. Its mission is to serve. It was initially founded in the late 1800s as a mutual aid society to assist Catholic immigrants new to the United States. There are nearly two million members worldwide, and many Catholic churches host chapters. The Knights of Columbus's small membership remains active at St. Ambrose Church, including organizing and

Knights of Columbus

cooking a church meal and aiding the church priest with the Corpus Christi procession. Their colorful regalia of sash, bright red or purple silk cape over a black suit, and a black hat boasting impressive white plumage distinguishes the Knights of Columbus when they perform their ceremonial roles.

The Holy Name Society invites men of St. Ambrose to join. They sponsor Boy Scout Troop 212 and raise funds for school scholarships. Similar to Holy Name societies in other local parishes, it is an opportunity for community stewardship, networking, and camaraderie.

St. Ambrose Forever was founded by parents of current students and alumni as a "non-profit charity organization with the purpose to fund an endowment for the betterment and longevity of St. Ambrose Grade School in St. Louis City." Through fundraisers and events, they established the Monsignor Bommarito Endowment Fund for families needing tuition assistance. It is a newer organization, having been formed in the 21st century, yet it possesses the same qualities as the community organizations that preceded it: a commitment to service and a dedication to sustaining a healthy, viable neighborhood.

Corpus Christi street altar

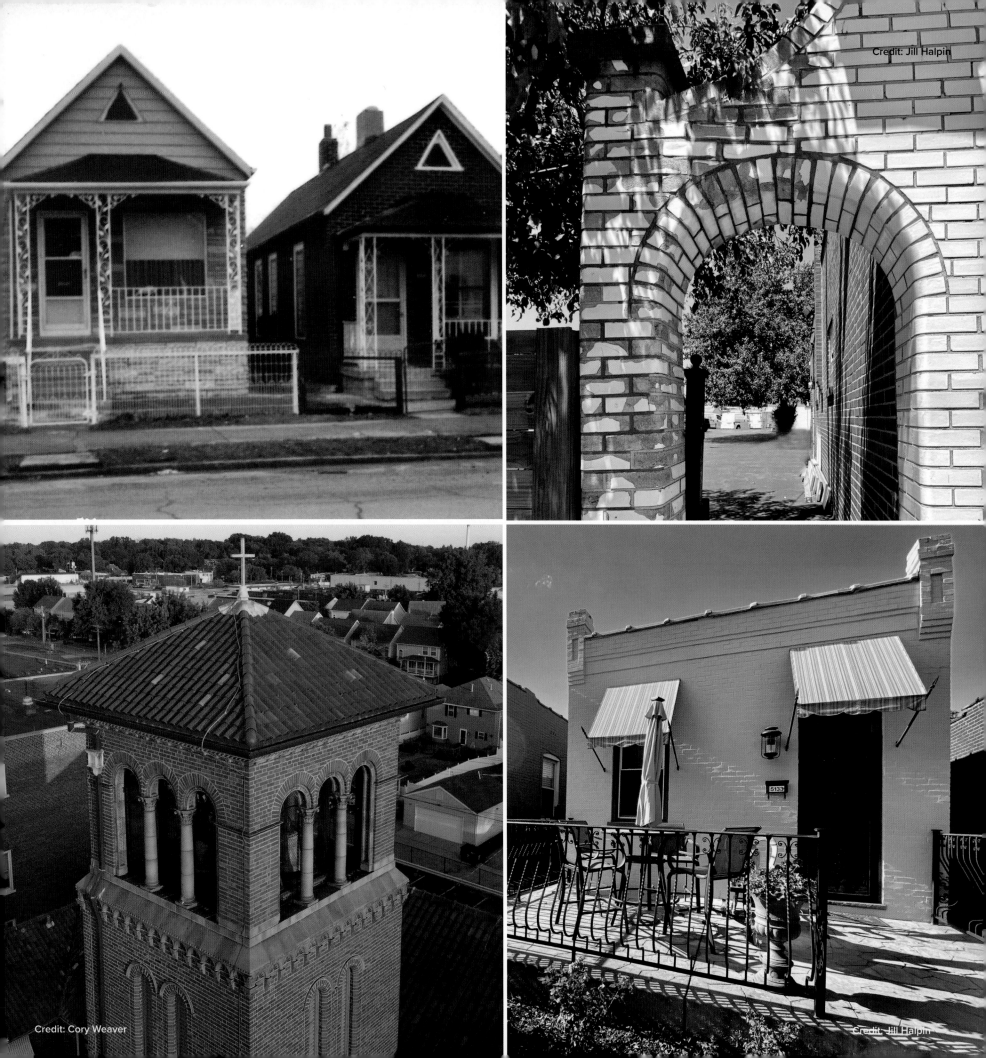

Credit: Jill Halpin

Credit: Cory Weaver

Credit: Jill Halpin

HOMES, BUILDINGS, AND ARCHITECTURE

The Hill's built spaces chronicle its history and reflect the enduring qualities of the neighborhood: stability and dynamism. The limited space between homes reflects its early history of working class immigrant frugality. Building material choices also evolved to become sturdier, more expensive, and later, more environmentally friendly. Because The Hill is zoned as a mixed-use neighborhood, what was once a business has been transformed into a home, and the reverse is true also. As older buildings were remodeled or replaced, architectural style mirrored the decades in which they were built. If visiting The Hill in person, take the time to explore. It will be hard to find just one favorite.

GENERATIONS LIVING IN THE SAME HOUSE

A common sentiment on The Hill is that it can be annoying to live here because everybody knows your business. It can also be a great place to live because everybody knows your business. The neighborhood knows when someone has gotten ill, passed, or experienced misfortune. The resulting hospital visits, funeral attendees, and general sympathy with offers to help are both welcome and overwhelming. A person is never alone in a time of need.

Community involvement stems from a neighborhood-wide institutional memory of large families sharing small homes, typically three-room shotgun houses. In addition to one extended family living in a house, it was common to take in boarders. They were generally single men having just arrived from Italy and either related to or from the same village as the homeowner. The custom helped alleviate the stressful transition into American life. Families took in orphans and the children of neighbors who did not have enough to feed them. Two or three generations of families sometimes lived in the same house or inhabited two houses next to each other. Familial lines were blurred. Grandparents, aunts, and uncles often had the same authority as parents, and children moved fluidly between the two homes.

The shotgun-style home became a hallmark of Hill architecture. House plots were long and narrow in order to reduce taxes, which were assessed on the width of a house. A family could begin with two rooms and add on to the back when savings and the number of children grew. The rooms were added on in a row, with no interior hallway. One had to pass through each intervening room to get from the back to the front. There was little expectation of privacy, and rooms were always shared.

Credit: Jill Halpin

Because Fairmount was initially remote, water and sewage systems came late. In the meantime, families built an outhouse on the back of the property near the alley. In the local vernacular it was called the "baccausu" (or back of the house), a term that still lingers today. The shotgun houses did have basements for tenants and often for cool sleeping quarters and a kitchen. Once utilities arrived on The Hill, the toilet was brought inside and the kitchen moved upstairs.

Shotgun houses still stand on The Hill, though they are being replaced by new property owners choosing to tear down the old and put in a new house on the same footprint as the shotgun. They build up two and even three stories to increase living space.

Roughly half of The Hill's new occupants are not from the neighborhood, or even Italian. Yet they spent a good sum to build a new home, thereby investing in the community. The other half are grandchildren and great-grandchildren of families that arrived in the early 1900s. Their parents went to St. Ambrose in the 1950s and 60s, yet when they graduated from college or trade school they could not settle in the community because the housing supply was so short, in part because their own parents were living into their 90s. It is encouraging to see a new generation of Italian Americans coming home to The Hill.

The houses on The Hill do stand uniformly, jutting at a strict perpendicular angle from true east–west or north–south streets. There is generally a standard distance between house and street. The house plots are narrow and long, usually 32 feet wide by 95 feet deep. Once established, this pattern is nearly impossible to change unless one purchases an entire block. Many have tried, but none have succeeded.

Homes on The Hill were built in phases adapting to current circumstances. The early houses on the northeastern portion of The Hill were constructed with wood. As brick became more affordable to those making it, houses might have a brick facade with wood sides. The 1904 World's Fair yielded mountains of deconstructed building materials that were eagerly carted away to adjacent neighborhoods. The post–World War II GI Bill funded homes west of Macklind. Population pressure and growing wealth drove a constant if uneven housing boom until the 1970s, when all but a few vacant lots were filled. In the 21st century, some older homes began to deteriorate beyond repair, yet those wishing to rebuild were generally stuck in the same footprint. Because of the geological makeup, some houses sit high off the street while others are only a few steps elevated. The underlying clay beds and streams challenge structural integrity. New home builders found that they had to pier their base floor deep into bedrock in order to maintain the building's integrity over the upcoming decades. Other homeowners chose to renovate their 100-year-old homes by adding extensions and moving interior walls to suit the modern lifestyle.

The houses that were constructed before 1970 were a tale of function over form. When walking the neighborhood, one can see two-family flats with two distinct living quarters. This made sense to the extended immigrant family, or to the family needing boarders for extra income. Four-family flats, tiny bungalows, long shotguns, and two separate houses on one plot are still represented.

While committed to function, The Hill's builders valued quality workmanship and aesthetic beauty. Decorative brickwork highlights the variations in the colors of clay pulled from the mines directly underneath. Glazed bricks enhance porches and facades. Wrought-iron fences establish gentle markers between properties. White terra-cotta embellishments such as pineapples or artichokes (both good luck symbols) grace the rooflines or buildings. Roman-themed designs in terra-cotta grace doorways and porticos. To perceive The Hill as a neat row of uniform shotgun houses is superficial; it just takes discernment to see adaptation and originality.

Street Names

There's a story behind just about everything on The Hill, and our street names are no exception. Charles Gratiot received a league square land grant from the Spanish government in 1798 amounting to a three-square-mile plot of land extending westward from Kingshighway. The Gratiot League Square was divided into the Fairmount and Cheltenham districts, and later the Gratiot heirs sold the land after separating it into thirteen parallel parcels, each extending east to west. William Sublette owned the Rocky Mountain Fur Company and was a competitor to John Jacob Astor's American Fur Company. Parcels within Sublette's land were owned by Mary Cooper. Cooper Street was renamed Marconi Avenue in 1938 after Guglielmo Marconi, inventor of the wireless telegraph. Others owning parcels in the Sublette estate were Margaret Wilson, the Hereford family, and Ashley Northrup, all represented by attorney W. E. Boardman.

W. C. Daggett owned the Fairmount district in partnership with William Phare, his trustee Elizabeth Phare, and Bernard Luetkemeyer. He named a street Bernard Street, but when the German immigrants arrived they changed the name to Bischoff, honoring German physiologist Theodor Bischoff.

Derrick January and John D. Dalton owned the Cheltenham district west of Sublette. St. Louis Heights, the subdivision south of Cheltenham, belonged to Samuel Reber and Robert Pattison.

Macklind Avenue used to be St. Louis Avenue, while Southwest was called Old Manchester after the current, straighter Manchester was completed. Berra Park and Berra Court are named in honor of Louis "Midge" Berra, a local politician who was fiercely devoted to the well-being of The Hill community.

Joe Garagiola, Lawrence "Yogi" Berra, Ben Pucci, and Jack Buck all resided on the 5400 block of Elizabeth Avenue, now renamed "Hall of Fame Place."

Former alderman Robert Ruggeri and exemplary Hill citizen Charlie "Schwaz" Milani have streets named after them in the new La Collina housing development.

Joe Garagiola (*left*) and Yogi Berra (*right*) at the ceremony for the renaming of Elizabeth Ave. to Hall of Fame Place.

Credit: Barbara Northcott

Credit: Cory Weaver

CHURCHES AND SCHOOLS

Faith and family are the foundation of any healthy community. Though St. Ambrose Catholic Church and School are considered the center of The Hill, other notable schools and churches flourished and served the neighborhood.

ST. AMBROSE CHURCH

 In 1902, there were two churches serving Italian immigrants in St. Louis: Our Lady Help of Christians at 10th and Wash Streets and St. Charles Borromeo at Locust and 29th Streets. The closest Roman Catholic Church to the Fairmount district was in the German community a couple blocks south of Fairmount. St. Aloysius Gonzaga was built in 1896, though it took several years to build the entire church structure.

Father Caesar Spigardi tended to the two Italian churches nearer to the river and established a mission for Fairmount's Italian community in the basement of St. Aloysius. Spigardi was able to raise funds from the community quickly and purchased a parcel of land on Cooper (Marconi) and Wilson Streets from an agent of the Anheuser-Busch Company. A new wooden-frame church, St. Ambrose, soon welcomed its own congregation in 1903 and became a focal point for most community activities.

Father Luciano Carotti, Father Spigardi's former assistant, became the pastor of the fully independent St. Ambrose Church in 1907. He focused on the church's construction debt, but he also spent money on a grade school for children of The Hill. Using his own two-room residence, he made two classrooms where students received up to a fifth-grade education.

Sometimes faith is tested by being asked to work harder than before even though you feel you have nothing left. The wooden St. Ambrose caught fire and burned to the ground in January 1921. Fortified by faith in God and each other, and through Father Carotti's leadership, every household took on the financial responsibility to rebuild a new

St. Aloysius Gonzaga

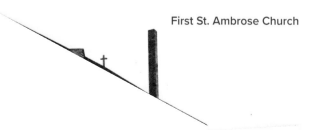

First St. Ambrose Church

St. Ambrose. Families were asked to pay at least $1 per month for five years, after which they would receive a certificate of merit. Though some families contributed considerably more funds, the entire neighborhood could claim ownership of a piece of the church. Grade-school children participated as well. After they accumulated $1 through chores or work, they donated it and would have a star painted on the church ceiling. Naturally, children had to be reminded not to rubberneck during mass (during the last repainting, one single star replaced the many).

The Hill community asked questions, learned details of the plans, and contributed their opinions in general meetings regarding the construction of the new church. They helped to pay for its construction and adornment. They owned it as much as they owned their homes. Visitors remark that The Hill is a close community, and the new St. Ambrose Church and School provides some insight into the neighborhood's foundation.

Architect Angelo Corrubia designed St. Ambrose using the Basilica of St. Ambrose in Milan, Italy, as inspiration. He used the same brick and terra-cotta that built The Hill neighborhood, reinforcing the idea that the church belongs to the people. The design is Lombard Romanesque. The new church cost $150,000 and seats over 400.

Four of the five church bells were donated from former hometowns in Italy. Cuggiono's bell honored its patron saint, Our Lady of Mount Carmel. Inveruno's honored St. Theresa, Marcallo's was dedicated to St. Nazario, and Casteltermini's to St. Vincent Ferreri. The fifth bell, from the people of the parish, honored St. Ambrose.

Father Julius Giovannini, pastor at the time of construction, donated altar vessels, candle standards, and new priestly vestments for the whole year, all from his personal savings.

On June 27, 1927, Archbishop John Glennon dedicated the new St. Ambrose. Mass followed, and then a daylong celebration ensued, complete with ravioli, a grand picnic, music, and dancing in the churchyard.

Guardian Angel

St. Ambrose Church

In the 1980s, *The Italian Immigrants* statue received loving maintenance and a makeover with a deep cleaning, bronze coating, and a new base.

St. Ambrose Church leaders and pastors have continued to personalize the church with chapels dedicated to Our Lady of Sorrows and Calgary. Saints representing the community adorn the walls between stained glass windows. They depict patron saints for the church community, the holy family, stations of the cross, and specific altars for the needy, ill, and unborn.

In 1972, the newest representation of The Hill's immigrant experience arrived. A seven-foot bronze statue designed by St. Louisan Rudolph (Rudy) Torrini called *The Italian Immigrants* was unveiled in front of St. Ambrose. It depicts a young immigrant couple of the early 1900s newly arrived in the United States. The woman holds a small baby tightly to her chest while the man has an immigration tag pinned to his lapel. While she looks tentative, even fearful, he has one foot forward and his chin is up, showing his determination to make the most of his new home. Torrini knew the story well, as his parents had traveled from Italy to America. It is our narrative, depicted in bronze.

Monsignor Vincent Bommarito is the longest-serving priest and pastor at St. Ambrose. The Hill's stability is bolstered by his loyalty and commitment to the community. Led by Monsignor Bommarito, Hill residents and benefactors demonstrated pride in their culture and community through the installation of Piazza Imo—another piece of Italy settling in a new home.

The symbiotic relationship between the parishioners and priests at St. Ambrose reflects the depth and breadth of the community as a whole. Our priests showed compassion and vision coupled with financial savvy. They rallied a community to invest in and build a brick church to replace a wooden one in four short years. The priests understood community relations and diplomacy. They also recognized when it was necessary to take a passionate stand to preserve the community, even if it meant taking the fight to Washington DC to mitigate the damage Interstate 44 caused when it cut off the north side of The Hill. They knew the value of guiding and nurturing neighborhood children by focusing their energies toward sport, community involvement, and education. While St. Ambrose Church serves a foundational role for The Hill, the parish priests maintain the bedrock.

THE ITALIAN IMMIGRANTS

ST. AMBROSE SCHOOL

St. Ambrose Parochial School registered its first students—50 boys and 50 girls—at 2110 Cooper Street in 1906. Father Carotti, assistant priest to Father Spigardi and promoted to parish pastor in 1907, managed fundraising and construction. The original wooden-frame school consisted of two rooms: a classroom for first through fourth grades and an auditorium that served as a multipurpose facility for meetings and special events.

From its humble beginnings, St. Ambrose Parochial School grew to be one of the finest grade schools in the city of St. Louis. In five years, by 1912, student enrollment doubled to 200. The increase is credited to Miss Margaret B. Eager, who taught at the school for 30 years, retiring in 1940. The nuns had a profound influence as well. Their combination of tough discipline and enduring love for their students created hard-working, motivated adults, loyal to family and community. From 1916 to 1919, the Order of St. Theresa sisters taught at St. Ambrose. After realizing St. Louis's brutally cold winters and sweltering summers posed health threats to the unacclimated, they were replaced by the Sisters of Loretto, who served until 1941. They were in turn followed by the Missionary Zelatrice Sisters of the Sacred Heart, who serve today as the Sisters of the Sacred Heart.

The population on The Hill exploded in the 1920s. National immigration laws had not yet restricted the flow of people from Italy, allowing extended families and village neighbors to be near each other again. By 1916, the St. Louis Archdiocese requested that St. Ambrose expand their curriculum to finish eighth grade. With the addition of older grade levels along with the population growth, St. Ambrose reached capacity and was forced to turn away thousands of potential students who then attended Shaw School, a city of St. Louis public school, instead.

The first formal school board formed in 1935. As part of the preparation for this new position, fifteen professional businessmen had to learn about curriculum and teaching methods, choirs, athletics, tournaments, and fundraising—both at the "corporate" level and through children's plays or other

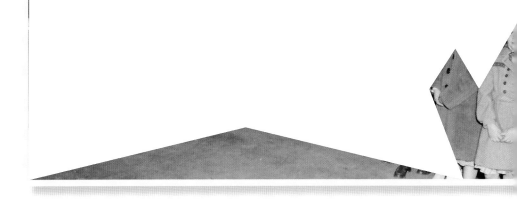

Father Palumbo receives Zenith Victrola from the choir.

talent shows. They learned about costs of books and supplies for students and teachers. Though different from planning co-ops or keeping public order, this task proved equally essential and really no different. It was a community effort led by those who were capable and willing in order to enrich the neighborhood.

Two rooms were added to the old structure in 1941. The enrollment outgrew it immediately. And, now that the school had a first through eighth grade, St. Ambrose's leadership was preparing students to succeed in—and graduate from—high school. Though the board hoped to start building an entirely new school in 1943, World War II delayed those plans. The new St. Ambrose was completed in 1949.

The school's curriculum and activities continue to change with the times. Today, the pre-K through eighth grade institution excels in athletics, building on the school's history of city championships in soccer and volleyball. The science, technology, engineering, and mathematics (STEM) program promises to earn a similar record of excellence.

Just as St. Ambrose Church is an anchor steadying the community through changes and challenges, the grade school serves a similar function. The annual Alumni Breakfast beckons former students ranging from high school freshmen to those celebrating their 75th graduation anniversary. Former students from as far as either coast make an effort to come home to catch up with old mates. Those attending pick up conversations where they left off, chatting with a familiarity that belies the fact

Opposite page: St. Ambrose's second school, which the community quickly outgrew

that they might not have seen each other in a year or more. Additionally, those who recently retired from their careers have time to renew bonds and make a point to get together once a month. Frequently a graduating class adopts a charity or cause related to The Hill, such as a donation to the Piazza in memory of a recently passed teacher or priest.

Illustration of St. Ambrose School

O'FALLON TECHNICAL HIGH SCHOOL

O'Fallon Technical High School opened in 1956 on McRee Avenue on the northwest side of The Hill. It was renamed **Gateway Institute of Technology** before becoming the **Gateway STEM High School** in 2012. It is the largest high school in the St. Louis Public School system, educating more than 1000 students in the sciences, technology, engineering, and math. In 2013 Gateway received attention from the Clinton Global Initiative University at Washington University through a William J. Clinton Foundation program started in 2007. The program connects university students to projects designed to teach future leaders how to tackle current global challenges such as providing technical skills to underserved populations.

St. Ambrose School Board *First row*: Louis J. Berra, Paul Calcaterra, David Fontana, Charles Garavaglia, John Barale, John Russo *Second row*: Louis J. Gualdoni, Paul Berra, Henry Ruggeri, Caesar Gioia, Father F. Lupo *Third row*: Charles Clavenna, Louis Visconti, John Clavenna

CHELTENHAM ELEMENTARY SCHOOL

An African American community consisting of freed slaves and free-born families lived in the Cheltenham and Fairmount districts before the German, Irish, and Italians settled in the area. Many within the community owned land, were skilled craftsmen, and were highly educated. Between 1877 and 1908, the Cheltenham Colored School or Colored School #10 served African American children living in The Hill area. Originally located in Cheltenham on Davis Street, the school moved to 5324–26 Northrup Avenue in Fairmount. In 1890, the board of education renamed the school Vashon after George Boyer Vashon and his son John B. Vashon, a principal of the school. In 1903, George Vashon instituted courses for girls, offering instruction in languages, letters and correspondences, and penmanship. Both men earned advanced degrees, and the father-son team publicly and frequently fought for educational and political opportunities for the African American community.

After the move, the school grew to 89 students at its peak in 1892. By 1908, the St. Louis Board of Education had closed the school, along with others in St. Louis, due to revenue shortfalls.

The Cheltenham School is now a private residence.

The properties were sold to generate income. The city opened a high school in the central part of the city in 1927, naming it Vashon High School. The school is still open today and remains a high-quality institution in athletics and academics.

SACRED HEART VILLA

The Sacred Heart Villa and Day Nursery at Wilson and Macklind was built in 1940. An order of nuns, the Apostles of the Sacred Heart of Jesus, opened and continue to operate the kindergarten. After scouting for a suitable place to build, they settled on the southeast corner of Wilson and Macklind. The large parcel of land was occupied by the Gambaro family, who agreed to move their house (on rollers) eastward so the Villa could be built. Architect Angelo Corrubia, who also designed St. Ambrose Church, oversaw construction. The Villa began childcare services with an enrollment of 12 in January 1940. In 1949, the Sisters authorized

Images of Sacred Heart Villa

Coronamento

Midge Berra speaks to the Villa's graduation class in the same year his son graduated. *Above right*: Children playing on Villa grounds.

construction of a holy grotto for Mary at which the community was invited to recite the rosary with the nuns every night in May and October. The grotto was repaired and refurbished in 1998, just in time for its 50th anniversary. It remains today as a beautiful reminder of faith, devotion, and community. Additionally, the May Crowning tradition continues to honor the Blessed Mother.

After working with St. Ambrose Grade School educators for 14 years, the Villa leaders started a girl's high school in the Villa building. The daycare moved to an adjacent house, and Cor Jesu Academy occupied the main building from 1956 to 1965. When enrollment grew too large, the academy moved to its current location on Gravois. The Villa's numbers expanded as well. In 1969, the kindergarten grew with a new addition built by a Hill resident and contractor.

Today, the Sacred Heart Villa continues to operate at full capacity. Its reputation for excellence reaches beyond The Hill as parents from all over the metropolitan area enroll

their children in the venerable institution. The Villa enjoys a loyalty stemming from legacy. Families from The Hill can recount attending the Villa through three or even four generations. A few of the Sisters claim the same longevity. Sister Felicetta Cola embodied the Villa's mission, inspiring three generations of children with her energetic and cheerful devotion. She even made pasta for the school by hand! Recently reassigned Sister Jude Ruggeri jubilantly steered the Villa through overhauls of curriculum delivery and the increased use of lay staff, as well as the challenges of maintaining the 80-year-old building. These two women represent all the dedicated teachers and staff, lay and religious alike, who have contributed and continue to contribute their inestimable service to the community.

Sister Felicetta (*left*) and **Sister Jude** (*right*)

Shaw School students' summer break parade

HENRY SHAW PUBLIC SCHOOL

The Henry Shaw public school was first opened in 1870 in a two-story frame building at Kingshighway and Vandeventer Avenue. It contained four rooms and had a capacity of 240 pupils. The present Shaw School at 5329 Columbia Avenue, designed by William B. Ittner, opened in 1907 with 928 pupils. In 1976, Shaw School joined the magnet program specializing in visual and performing arts and two years later became a community education center. Three hundred fifty students ranging from preschool through fifth grade attend the school annually.

In keeping with national trends in desegregated education, today most Shaw Visual and Performing Arts Elementary School students come to the school from neighborhoods miles away. In earlier decades, students walked or were carpooled to school from St. Ambrose and other nearby parish neighborhoods. Just as St. Ambrose grappled with getting enough space to house a

growing student body, other parish schools experienced a similar situation. Additionally, The Hill and surrounding neighborhoods had families who did not have the means to send their offspring to a parochial school that charged even a seemingly nominal tuition. In the pre–World War II decades, children started working by the time they finished fifth grade, having learned to read and do math—the only competencies necessary for menial labor.

Such was the norm for the first generation of immigrant children born in the United States. They straddled the old and the new and navigated through the tides and eddies. However, Shaw School graduates from The Hill maintained the old traditions by identifying with their graduating class, holding reunions, and keeping in touch, just like their St. Ambrose counterparts.

Shaw Community Activity Center

The Henry Shaw public school became a community activity center in the 1950s, receiving city funds to enrich its neighborhood. It offered after-school children's programming, summer activities for children in the school and at Sublette and Berra Parks, as well as an eclectic mix of choices for adults including Italian-language classes, crafts classes, and music and dance lessons.

Always an active institution, in 1910 Henry Shaw School students petitioned the school board for a wading pool in their schoolyard for summer use. After other grade schools joined the petition, pools were installed in several public grade schools across the city. Unfortunately, all public pools in St. Louis closed in July 1949 due to the polio epidemic. Even as the St. Louis Public School District faces challenges, Shaw School continues to participate in community activities. The school gym serves as an election polling station and the schoolyard is the stage for the annual car show.

Credit: Jill Halpin

Credit: Jill Halpin

MEN'S GARMENTS
2 Pc. SUITS· .90
3 Pc. SUITS· 1.00
PANTS· .45
TOPCOATS· 1.00
OVERCOATS· 1.25
TIES· .15
SWEATERS· .50
SHORT JACKETS· .65 up
ROBES· 1.00 up
SHIRTS· .50
P-COATS· .85
LEATHER-JACKETS 3.00
MEN'S HATS· .75
CHILDREN'S GARM
3 Pc. SNOW-SUIT 1.00 up
2 Pc. SNOW-SUIT .85 up
COATS .50 up

LAD
DRES
2 Pc.
LONG
FUR T
SHORT
BLOU
JUMP
SKIRT
RAINC
WATER
ROBES
SLAC
SWEA
PANTS
SKIRT
SHORT

Bertarelli CUTLERY
Sharpening Services
Kitchen Supplies

Credit: Jill Halpin

FOOD, SHOPS, AND BUSINESSES

Because the Italian immigrant settlement that became The Hill was five miles from the St. Louis riverfront and commerce, the growing enclave learned to be self-sufficient. The immigrants and their children built businesses to provide for every need of an expanding community. Local small businesses such as hair styling, legal and realty services, construction, funeral services, boutiques, and e-commerce thrive, and family-owned restaurants, delis, bakeries, and groceries have grown to accommodate residents and visitors alike.

Credits: Barbara Northcott

GUIDO'S
PIZZERIA
Y TAPAS

The Hill

PIT STOP

grazie
TO ALL
FRONTLINE
WORKERS

RESTAURANTS

The Hill offers over two dozen eateries in less than a square mile. The majority are Italian themed, though **Guido's** includes Spanish tapas, reflecting the family's Spanish heritage. Likewise, **Anthonino's** menu combines Italian dishes alongside Greek favorites, paying homage to the chef/owner brothers' Greek Italian ancestry. **Carnivore,** and its event space **D'Amici Room, J. Smugs GastroPit**, and **Pit Stop** offer steaks, barbecue, and a multifaceted menu, respectively. They are newer to The Hill, expanding the Smugala family and partners' St. Louis–area restaurant collection.

5101

Dominic's

Lou Boccardi's daughter runs the family's Italian eclectic eatery. The Saracino family has operated restaurants on The Hill since the mid-1950s. The first Bartolino's moved and became **Bartolino's Osteria** on Hampton, while **Chris' Pancakes** operates just two blocks off The Hill and is one of two family-owned restaurants in the neighborhood serving breakfast. The old Bartolino's became the popular **Joey B's**, offering large portions and amazing salads. While you may experience fine dining plus an opera performance at **Dominic's**, **Lorenzo's** creates delicious unique Northern Italian dishes.

Credit: Jill Halpin

Credit: Barbara Northcott

The Place in St. Louis for Pasta

Cunetto

HOUSE OF PASTA

5453 Magnolia

Credit: Cory Weaver

Charlie Gitto's often hosts local celebrities who are drawn to quality cuisine, and **J. Devoti's** specializes in innovative, farm-to-table, nose-to-tail Italian cooking. Not to be "out-chefed," **Gian-Tony's** excels in Southern Italian specialties, as does another brothers' restaurateur establishment, **Favazza's**. Family-friendly restaurants include well established **Zia's**, **Mama's** (which claims the invention of toasted ravioli in rivalry with Charlie Gitto's), and **Cunetto's**, operated by a family of pharmacists turned restaurateurs since 1972. Cunetto's offers Northern Italian dishes and serves Muny Opera enthusiasts and professional sports fans on game days. **LoRusso's** rounds out The Hill menu with superbly prepared Italian classics.

Mama's "ON THE HILL"

Credit: Jill Halpin

Famous Homemade Hot Salami
—SINCE 1918—
GIOIA'S DELI
776-9410

Credits: Jill Halpin

The following establishments are especially notable. Gioia's Market, now Gioia's Deli, was opened in 1918 by the Gioia brothers. The Donley family bought the grocery in 1980, and have grown the business in quantity and quality. **Gioia's Deli** won a James Beard Foundation America's Classics Award in 2017. The national award honors dining establishments that are locally owned, have been in business for more than ten years, and serve quality food that reflects the character of the community. The lunch lines for Gioia's delicious signature cooked hot salami sandwiches typically spill out the door.

Rigazzi's is the oldest continuously operating restaurant on The Hill run by the same family that opened it. They offer large home-cooked portions and the only "fishbowl" or schooner of beer, while overnight shift workers appreciate Rigazzi's hearty breakfast. It is a favorite for fans heading to a Cardinals or Blues game. Nostalgic diners enjoy the sports, music, and Hollywood memorabilia hugging every inch of wall space.

Credit: Jill Halpin

Sala's operated from 1911 to 1976 and was one of the first restaurants on The Hill. The memory of Sala's ham and beef sandwiches still makes some seniors on The Hill go "hmmm." In its early years, the restaurant offered curbside service for women in carriages as they waited for their husbands who were socializing in the men's-only tavern.

Today, the restaurant has a new life as Oliva, an event space and catering business that specializes in wedding receptions, offers suites for overnight guests, and has an outdoor patio cocktail hour and a semi-attached antique consignment mall. The refurbished building gives testimony to original early 20th-century craftsmanship. The nationally known **Ruggeri's Restaurant**, which was founded around the time of the 1904 World's Fair by Antonio Ruggeri and closed in 1982, hosted numerous celebrities, including Rat Pack pals, sports legends, and newscasters. But the celebs were not the only ones who could sing; the waiters burst into velvety baritone renditions of "Volare" or "O Solo Mio" whenever the mood struck. Mickey Garagiola, Joe's brother, was one of the tuxedo-clad servers at Ruggeri's for decades. Today, the younger Ruggeri's waitstaff, those in their 60s and 70s, meet for lunch once a month. The building is now known as **The Rose of The Hill** and serves as the only large event venue in the community.

Ruggeri's busboys

Ruggeri's 1956

SALA'S CAFE
STEAKS and SEA FOODS
PARKING

Credit: Jill Halpin

FOOD AND MORE: SPEND A DAY ON THE HILL

Credits: Jill Halpin

Food isn't the center of life on The Hill, it's just how we pass the day. Delicious and unique food draws customers from the metro area and the entire region every weekend. People will make a day trip to The Hill. They may have a coffee at bank-turned-coffeehouse **Shaw Coffee** and then stroll to the **Missouri Baking Company** (Missouri Bakery) or **Vitale's Bakery** to find a traditional Italian pastry, or cookies, or cake, or muffins, and, yes, cannoli. Adventurous cooks may buy fresh dough to make pizzas at home, or they may opt for a premade pizza shell that simply needs toppings and baking.

The **Hill Neighborhood Center** is the perfect place to plan your day. Learn about Hill history, get a map of the neighborhood and a souvenir t-shirt, or join a lively conversation with Hill residents. A trip to **Berra Park** is always a treat on Saturdays and Sundays. The park hosts festivals and soccer and softball tournaments as well as weeknight league games. Pickup soccer is a weekend staple, where experienced players display the remarkable talent The Hill is known for. A walk down a few of the neighborhood streets offers a chance to see our unique architecture. As The Hill is experiencing a revival, older

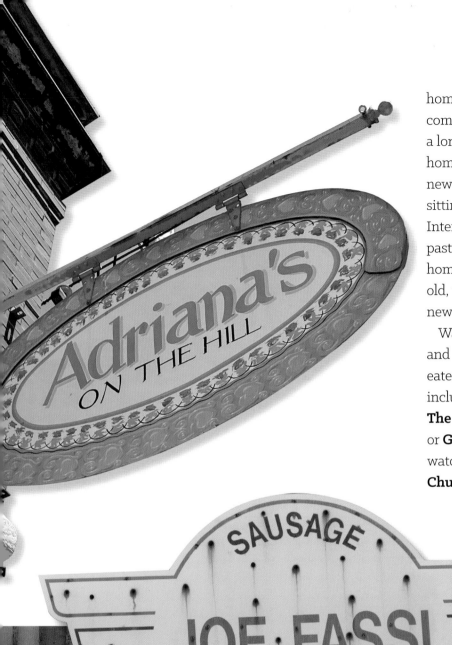

homes are either being torn down or completely renovated. What was once a long row of neat, well-maintained homes has become a showcase of new personal architectural expression sitting next to antique homes. Interestingly, the spirit of The Hill's past asserts itself as many of the new homes are built on the footprint of the old, thus maintaining the old order yet with new faces.

Walking the neighborhood works up an appetite, and the visitor is spoiled for choice. Perhaps a sandwich at one of our many eateries . . . but deciding among the many options can be difficult. Delis include **Toscano's**, **Eovaldi's**, **Adriana's**, **Charlie Imo's Deli & Market on The Hill**, **Southwest Market**, and **Joe Fassi's**. After lunch, visit **Cafe Dolce** or **Gelato di Riso** next to **Piazza Imo**, and enjoy the fountain and people-watching. There might even be a wedding party on the steps of **St. Ambrose Church**. Next, wander the area to visit local shops.

Credit: Jill Halpin

Bertarelli
CUTLERY
Sharpening Services
Kitchen Supplies

Credit: Cory Weaver

Head north to Pattison using the pedestrian walkway over Highway 44 to visit **Chocolate, Chocolate, Chocolate**, and take a tour of their yummy factory. **Pop's Blue Moon** might have a live band on a Saturday afternoon. Come back to watch handmade soap being crafted at **Herbaria**, or have a custom bling shirt made at **Daily Disco** after getting some flowers at **City House Country Mouse**. Shop for unique fashions at **KoHo Clothing and Accessories** or antiques at **David Kent Richardson's Decorations & Design** or **The Hill Antique Market**. **Bertarelli's** specializes in knife sharpening, but they also sell unique imported kitchen items.

Right: Chocolate, Chocolate, Chocolate
Below: Herbaria

Credit: Cory Weaver

Shop for Italian specialty groceries at **DiGregorio's** (grab a loaf of **Marconi Bakery** bread too), **Viviano's**, **Volpi's**, or **Urzi's**. All have unique offerings, and be sure to bring a cooler with you to take home refrigerated treasures.

Delizioso

ANTIQUE MARKET
THE HILL

It might be close to 5 p.m., just in time for the Saturday evening mass. Perhaps a break at **Milo's** before going for dinner at one of our (many, many) fabulous restaurants. Enjoy your meal and have a safe trip home or stay at an Airbnb. Or make it a full evening at the **Gaslight Lounge** where you can enjoy a live studio recording, open mic night, or a comedian.

Credit: Cory Weaver

What a Baker!

 Joann Gambaro Arpiani won an award in a national baking competition without having actually made the dessert first and was given her award by future president Ronald Reagan.

Credits: Jill Halpin

CHOCOLATE
BISCOTTI

BUTTER
CHOCOLATE CHIP

BUTTER

BAKERIES AND GROCERIES

MISSOURI BAKING COMPANY

 The Missouri Baking Company, or Missouri Bakery, opened in 1924 at the corner of Edwards and Wilson. It was founded by the Gambaro and Arpiani families who have owned and operated the bakery for four generations. They offer baked goods such as Italian specialty cookies, fruit stollen and Danish pastries, desserts like tiramisu, Italian bread and rolls, and even pizza dough ready to be topped and baked. Their famous chocolate drops tempt even the most disciplined, while seasonal breads and cakes such as a lamb-shaped Easter cake justify any indulgence.

VITALE'S BAKERY

 The Bommarito and Vitale families operate a three-generations-old bakery. Bommarito's Bakery at 18th and Madison Streets in downtown St. Louis opened in 1947. In 1976, after the Bommarito patriarch retired, his children moved the business to The Hill, renaming it Vitale's Bakery. The third generation operates the business today. Vitale's offers Italian cookies and pastries, and the bakery supplies businesses with pre-made pizza shells. They are known for their excellent cannoli and bread.

MARCONI BAKERY

In 1969, Sam Licata bought Marconi Bakery. He was a recent Italian immigrant instilled with the determination to work two jobs to raise his family of four. The bakery at 1913 Marconi had at least two owners prior to Licata. He retired after selling his business to the DiGregorio family in 2016. Though the business passed through unrelated hands, it remains a proud family business. Delicious Marconi bread is for sale to the public during bakery hours and at DiGregorio's Market thereafter.

FAZIO'S BAKERY

The delectable staff of life produced by the Fazio family has supplied St. Louis's restaurants for four generations. Through baker's hours, hard work, and a commitment to quality, the family-owned and operated business of over 80 years has a bright future. The Fazios offer artisanal bread at well-known farmers' markets across the city, enticing fans to try offerings such as sourdough, rye, pumpernickel, and asiago bread. Additionally, they have expanded into the specialty food business, including ready-made sauces and pastas.

AMIGHETTI'S BAKERY

In 1921, Italian immigrant Louis Amighetti Sr. moved his bakery to Wilson Avenue across the street from the emerging new St. Ambrose Church. His son, Louis "Junior" Amighetti, continued working the family business and baking phenomenal bread.

Amighetti's Bakery was woven into the fabric of everyday life on The Hill. Junior, in partnership with his wife, Marge, expanded the business with an internationally known sandwich called the Amighetti's Special.

As with the loss of any decades-old, generational friend, The Hill mourns the 2019 closing of Amighetti's Bakery.

URZI'S MARKET

Since 1926, three generations of the Urzi family have operated a familiar corner grocery store that constantly strives to meet the needs of their customers. Urzi's market offers sweet snacks, savory treats, wine, specialty canned goods, frozen dinner items such as seafood ravioli, and ingredients and specific tools to make your own lavish Italian meal. A quick tutorial from Diane, the Urzi matriarch, sets customers up to become spedini specialists or cannoli artists.

Credit: Jill Halpin

PIZZA
SALSICCIA
RAVIOLI
PASTA
MEAT BALLS
STOP AT URZI'S

URZI'S
ITALIAN
MARKET

EST. 1926

DIGREGORIO'S ITALIAN MARKET

Salvatore "Sam" DiGregorio opened DiGregorio's Italian Market in 1971. The store remains in the family with the operations in the hands of Sam's children, who are currently teaching their own kids how to run the business. DiGregorio's is renowned for the neat packaging of deli meats and cheeses sliced to order. They offer specialty Italy-sourced pastas, olive oils, vinegars, premium canned products, Italian coffee, and imported packaged deserts. The fresh meat counter offers superior options for a home-cooked meal. DiGregorio's Market can also supply the harried cook with delicious frozen quick dinner options from venison cutlets to gnocchi to lasagna.

mangia

Credits: Jill Halpin

VIVIANO AND SONS MARKET

The Viviano brothers, John and Tony, carry on the family business that their grandfather opened in 1950 and grew into a larger location in 1979. Viviano's carries aisles of pasta varieties plus wine to match. They offer a full-service deli for freshly sliced meats and sandwiches prepared to order. Olive oil, vinegars, and canned tomatoes imported from Italy inspire a cook, while imagining meals from the prepared sausage and meat cases makes the belly rumble. Viviano's is a lively place; be prepared for a wine tasting, a Saturday afternoon music session, or a jovial conversation among neighborhood friends.

Credit: Jill Halpin

LOCAL BUSINESSES SUSTAIN A COMMUNITY

Immigrants settled on The Hill in the late 1800s. At the time, the area was far from the St. Louis city center, lacking in basic necessities, and without public transportation. A trip to the city center and markets took a full day by horseback or wagon. The resourceful Italian enclave met its own needs by opening markets, shops, and saloons. That tradition remains today. Typically these businesses occupied a corner as opposed to being in the middle of a block, allowing businesses and residents to coexist. However, Marconi and Shaw Avenues have always been the "main streets" of The Hill. The same buildings housed subsequent tenants over the years, and each establishment's persona was shaped by its owner and the customers who frequented it. Parents taught their children which store to shop for a specific item. Many family dinner conversations revolved around whose salami was better and why, or where to get the best bread versus the best buns, or who gave better credit terms if buying a piece of furniture.

The tendency of residents to meet their needs locally extended to health care as well, so The Hill's healers have always played an important role in the community. Two trained and licensed midwives, Mrs. Maria Vopli and Mrs. Rosa Valli, delivered babies in the home and cared for mothers and babies well after the birth. Dr. Ira W. Upshaw, who lived on Shaw Avenue in the 1920s, was the ideal general practitioner, treating everything from bones broken in horse accidents to skin burnt in house fires. Dr. Charles Montani looms large in Hill seniors' memories as as a physician who stayed up to date on the most current medical knowledge but maintained a personal connection with his patients for generations.

Credit: Barbara Northcott

Leopold Oldani and his brothers George and Joseph founded Oldani Brothers' Sausage Company in 1946. Now under its third owner, the Salumeria continues to produce favored Genoa salami for Hill delis and for customers across the country.

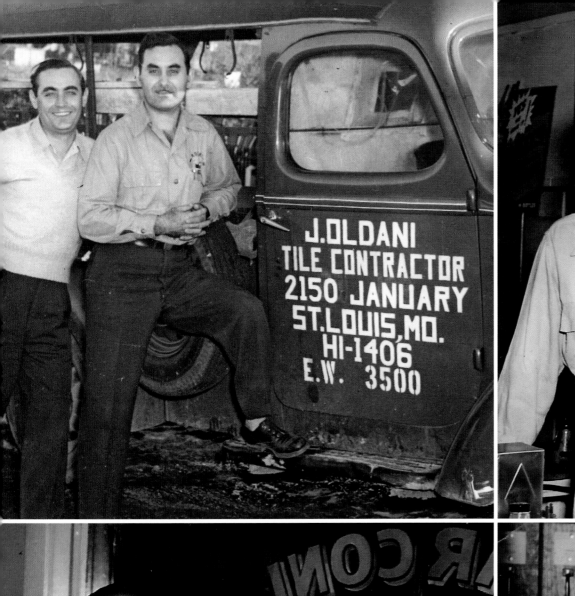

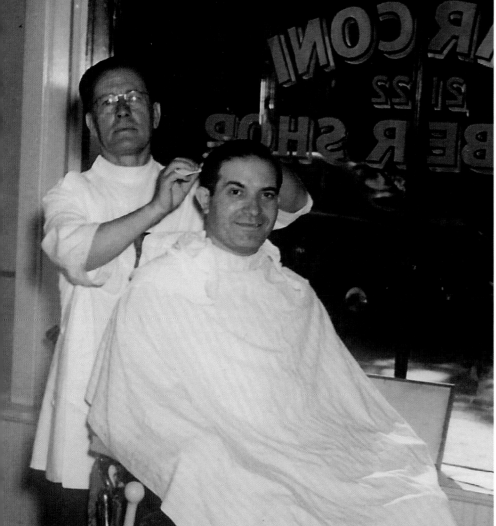

The partial list below was printed as a thank-you by Hill 2000 to supporting businesses in May 1971. While some of these businesses survive, many have closed.

The variety of businesses indicates a healthy retail environment in a neighborhood with a population of 3,000. In 1971, as in the previous decades, residents rarely left The Hill because they lived and worked there, and because the self-enclosed hamlet had everything they needed.

Today, family-owned businesses continue to thrive. While residents and restaurateurs may fuss over scarce parking, homeowners still believe the businesses come with the legacy of being part of the community.

Thank You

Amighetti's Bakery
Angelo's Restaurant
Berra Furniture
Berra Paint
Calcaterra's Funeral Home
Cassani's Restaurant
Columbia Theater
Colombo's Market
Connie Ann Florist
Consolino's Grocery Store
Cunetto's Pharmacy

DiGregorio's Market
Driftwood Tavern
Fair Mercantile Furniture and Appliances
Fairmount Service Station
Fairway Department Store
Fassi's Grocery Store
Gioia's Market
Hanneke Hardware
Leotta's Market
Missouri Baking Company
Oldani's Salami
Phyllis Florist
Ribaudo's Market
Rigazzi's Restaurant

Riggio's Realty Company
Ruggeri's Restaurant
Rumbolo's Market
Sala's Café
St. Ambrose Church
Joe Serra—Attorney
Southwest Bank
Spielberg Furniture
Style Craft Manufacturers
Toscano's Market
Wil-Mar Lounge
Venegoni's Huddle Lounge
Volpi's Salami

Galimberti's
Credit: Hill 2000 newsletter
October 1975

SPORTS AND RECREATION

Hill residents love their sports . . . a lot. While taking a summer stroll through the neighborhood, the voice of a Cardinals baseball game announcer wafts from radios on front porches. A neighborhood businessman painted his parade-loving antique firetruck St. Louis Blues blue, adorning it with a Stanley Cup replica to celebrate the Blues' 2019 victory. Hockey, soccer, and baseball fans are ubiquitous throughout The Hill, as are Kentucky Derby parties (hats required), Bocce leagues and tournaments, charity golf tournaments, bike races, a soap box derby, and softball, volleyball, and basketball leagues.

THE HILL WALK OF FAME

In 2002, Hill 2000 organized a Walk of Fame for residents whose achievements left an indelible mark on the history of The Hill. The honorees range from educators to athletes who committed themselves to excellence in their field and modeled a lifestyle of service to our community.

Hill 2000 commissioned bronze plaques placed in the carriage walks of the homes of the honorees. The memorials are scattered throughout The Hill, creating an informative Hill Historical Walk.

Fourteen plaques identify the following:

Joe Garagiola
5446 Elizabeth Avenue
St. Louis Cardinal, Today Show Anchor,
Guest Host Johnny Carson Tonight Show

Jack Buck
5405 Elizabeth Avenue
Professional Sports Announcer
and Interviewer

Lawrence "Yogi" Berra
5447 Elizabeth Avenue
New York Yankee, Ten Time World
Series winner

Frank "Pee Wee" Wallace
5119 Daggett Avenue
1950 USA World Cup Soccer Team

Gino Pariani
5108 Daggett Avenue
1950 USA World Cup Soccer Team

Charlie Colombo
5565 Elizabeth Avenue
1950 USA World Cup Soccer Team

Frank C. Borghi
1919 Marconi Avenue
1950 USA World Cup Soccer Team,
Funeral Director

Mickey Garagiola
5446 Elizabeth Avenue
Professional Wrestling Announcer,
Loyal Friend of The Hill

Ben Pucci
5430 Elizabeth Avenue
Professional Football Player (Cleveland)

Marie "Re" Calcaterra
2307 Edwards Street—Synchronized
Swimming Pioneer, Champion Coach,
Member of the International Swimming
Hall of Fame

Miss Rose Oldani
4949 Columbia Avenue
Organist, Choir Director and
Piano Teacher

Charlie Garavaglia
2129 Macklind Avenue
Musician, Founder of Italian Heritage
Program and Young Artists Competition

Sr. Felicetta Cola ASCJ
2108 Macklind Avenue
Teacher, Mentor, and Devoted Apostle
of the Sacred Heart of Jesus

Eleanore Berra-Marfisi
2005 Macklind Avenue
Teacher, Poet, Author and
Loyal Friend of The Hill

Mickey Garagiola

Shaw Park playground

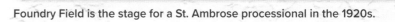
Foundry Field is the stage for a St. Ambrose processional in the 1920s.

LOCAL PARKS AND PLAYGROUNDS USED BY THE HILL COMMUNITY

 Because The Hill developed five miles from the center of St. Louis and the Mississippi riverfront, it was an ethnic enclave with large, undeveloped parcels of land that made for a variety of play places. When Shaw School opened at Macklind and Columbia in 1924, the city board of public education maintained a playground and large lot adjacent to the building. The city managed another small playground on the corner of Shaw and Boardman Avenues. A vacant field at Macklind and Wilson where the Sacred Heart Villa stands today served as an informal play place. The open area at Macklind and Shaw, known as Vigo Park, Macklind Field, or today's Berra Park, served the neighborhood initially as a community dump and semi-prohibited play place. It evolved into a community area for picnics, events, and informal soccer, baseball, softball, and corkball tournaments.

The largest area reached from Marconi to Kingshighway with Southwest at its southern border. Since it bordered the McQuay-Norris foundry, it was known as Foundry Field. Hill residents were delighted when famous circuses like Ringling Brothers and Barnum & Bailey came to town, setting up so close to home. Foundry Field hosted league play and tournaments for local soccer, baseball, and softball teams. For example, the YMCA leagues from the north and south sides of the city sent their best players for an annual all-city all-star softball game in the 1930s. Eventually the area was consumed by commercial property, another indicator of The Hill's economic growth.

BERRA PARK

Francis Vigo was a contemporary of George Rogers Clark, the frontier militia commander during the American Revolution. Vigo, born in 1747 in the north of what is now Italy in a town named Mondovi, made his way to the British colonies by way of a Spanish Army regiment stationed in New Orleans. He then made the new world his new home. He traded furs with native peoples and supported the American Revolution by loaning money and supplies. The British troops captured him then held him at their fort because he allied himself with the Spanish and Americans. They warned him to keep quiet about his experience in the British fort at Vincennes, in the Indiana territory, and released him. Vigo promptly stopped in St. Louis, his final destination according to the orders of his former captors, but then carried on to Kaskaskia in Illinois to supply Clark with intelligence on the British.

Vigo's posthumous presence was shorter lived on The Hill. In 1959, the St. Louis Parks and Recreation Department named the playfield at Shaw and Macklind Avenues Vigo Park. In 1965, the Parks Department renamed the area Berra Park in honor of Louis G. "Midge" Berra, the first Italian American to be elected to a citywide position (collector of revenue) in St. Louis. Visitors often erroneously assume Berra Park is named after baseball legend Lawrence "Yogi" Berra.

Yogi, like his contemporaries, called the area Macklind Field. From the early 1900s to the 1940s, Macklind Field served as a dump, not of the refuse sort, but as a place where items that had served a second or third or fourth life were discarded. They might be old glass jelly jars that became juice glasses, or old porcelain-covered metal gas station signs that became roofs for a clubhouse, or furniture with no last legs useful for making a campfire. But mostly the dumps were open fields where residents tossed coal ashes from stoves and furnaces. Mine shafts ran under the field, occasionally giving way and causing injury to children who disobeyed their parents' warnings to stay clear. Children and teens used Macklind Field to meet friends, watch and play ball games, take turns on the swings, escape from the small family house, and enjoy the annual festas. It bonded the community through fun, just as St. Ambrose bonded the community through faith.

Louis G. "Midge" Berra

BOCCE

Bocce (pronounced bow-chee on The Hill) dates back to 15th-century Italy. It is played on a lane of finely ground chat involving four balls per team and two teams. First a player tosses a smaller ball, called a *pallino*, or *boccin* (boo-cheen) down the lane. The players then roll a ball to get closest to the pallino, thereby earning points. In order to be competitive, players must be skilled at throwing the ball with precision and well-controlled force. They also use the banks of the lane to ricochet their shots in order to knock away or get behind a competitor's ball and closer to the pallino. After the eight balls are thrown to the end, the interesting part follows.

Players hover over the balls on the ground discussing which ball is closest, using animated body language to make their point. Players employ all sorts of measurement tools, including the obvious tape measure, yardstick, notched broom handle, even an old selfie stick.

Bocce is a staple on The Hill. Courts occupied tavern patios quickly after the Italians arrived. League play developed around

Credit: Jill Halpin

the 1940s so more people could enjoy the sport. Bocce leagues at Milo's Tavern & Bocce Garden draw players and spectators from all corners of The Hill. Spring, summer, and fall leagues encourage conviviality. Milo's hosts two annual charity tournaments in November and January, just to keep the muscle memory active! The Italia-America Bocce Club opened first on Manchester, then moved to its present location on Marconi. It is a members-only club. The Bocce Club courts are professional quality, which enables the organization to host well-attended national and international tournaments. Indeed, some Hill residents are so devoted to the game that they build courts in their backyards!

SOCCER

goal!

Whether the players learned the sport when they grew up in Italy or were mentored under Uncle Joe Causino's Y.M.C.A. club system, the Catholic Youth Council athletic program, or brothers in the backyard, The Hill's soccer talent often played as soon as they could walk. They earned the chance to play on an Olympic team, became college All-Americans, reigned as St. Louis City champions, participated in nationwide elite leagues, and played on professional indoor and outdoor teams. Numerous players are inductees into the St. Louis Soccer Hall of Fame. The Hill's soccer culture provides another network of players young and old who share a deeply cherished common experience. At the decades-old annual Turkey Bowl, Hill residents delight in watching pure talent having fun.

World Cup

From the perspective of a longtime Hill resident, the 1950 World Cup soccer match between England and the United States happened only yesterday (even if one was not yet born). An internet search reveals that sportswriters still rehash the game every four years, reminding readers of the remarkable upset.

The skilled English were experienced, superior players who played together as a team. The Americans were the opposite. Their team consisted of eleven starters who had not met each other nor played together until a few weeks before the World Cup matches—except for the five players from St. Louis who made the team. Four of the St. Louisans were from The Hill, where they had joined the athletic clubs on their street and played competitively since they were just tykes. Upon making the team, they left their day jobs as a funeral director, teacher, and mailman to play in Brazil.

Calling the game an upset is an understatement. The poised, polished English team showed contempt toward the Americans, believing them to be second-rate players from a country that barely recognized the game. The English forgot that the US is a nation of immigrants who embrace games of their old country and approach their work and sport with serious determination bordering on survival instinct. Not only were the English taken off guard, they simply had an unlucky day, and had to return home to explain how they lost, 1–0, to such a ragtag team.

During the World Cup match, the *New York Times* did not print the story because the editorial staff was convinced that the telegraph received from Brazil must have been a mistake and the actual score was 10–0 in England's favor. When the players arrived home at Lambert Field, only one reporter greeted them. In the following weeks, the story took its rightful place in the headlines. Decades later, a book written by Geoffrey Douglas called *The Game of their Lives* became the basis for a movie of the same name. The production team came to The Hill to film, making use of the streets, shops, church, and school as background. Hill residents eagerly played extras. The Hill's champions finally received appreciation for their accomplishment. For the rest of the community, sports continued, and life went on. The athletes went back to their jobs and blended back into their community, though each left an indelible mark.

LAWRENCE (YOGI) BERRA AND JOE GARAGIOLA

Lawrence, (Yogi) Berra and Joe Garagiola are staples of Hill history. Both men were born in the mid-1920s of Italian immigrant parents, fought in World War II, and rose to great heights in professional baseball. The best friends grew up across the street from each other, played for the New York Yankees and St. Louis Cardinals, respectively, developed excellence in their professions, and left an enduring legacy on American history. They are also testimonies to children of The Hill that greatness can be achieved from humble beginnings.

Lawrence—"Lawdy" to his contemporaries and "Yogi" to the rest of us—crafted an exemplary life from humble beginnings with determined talent and strength of character. He barely finished grade school, was unlikely in looks and dialogue, yet understood that passion and hard work would pay off. Berra enlisted to fight in World War II, surviving two landings at Normandy. He won ten World Series rings as a player and manager and was inducted into the Major League Baseball Hall of Fame. His baseball accomplishments set the foundation for

Yogi Berra, Chuck Diering, Joe Garagiola, Pete Reiser, and Red Schoendienst

Joe Garagiola

Bottom right, Joe and Yogi

Yogi Berra

the Yogi Berra Museum and Learning Center in New Jersey. Extended family members live in the Berra home on The Hill on Elizabeth Avenue, renamed Hall of Fame Place.

Joe Garagiola grew up on Elizabeth Avenue directly across the street from Lawdy Berra. They embarked on their baseball careers at the same time, going to trainings and tryouts together. Garagiola admits to being less talented on the baseball diamond than his buddy Berra, but he was no less an endearing character. Garagiola used the patois of his humble beginnings with an

elegance that charmed radio and television audiences. He walked off the field into the announcers' booth, broadcasting games locally and then nationally. He served as a host on NBC's *Today* show and a guest host on the *Johnny Carson Show*, and he also hosted the Westminster Dog show and TV game shows. However, his best appearances were reserved for the St. Ambrose Alumni Breakfasts.

Professional football player Ben Pucci and nationally known sports announcer Jack Buck also lived on Hall of Fame Place.

EVENTS

The elders born at the turn of the last century could often be heard telling their children or grandchildren who got too excited to "wait a while." Occasionally, even today that phrase spoken in the same manner causes those who remember to smile. It is a cautionary piece of advice to assess the situation, then plan how to deal with it. Keep what works, change what is necessary to keep the community healthy, and help each other out. The Hill endured two world wars, Prohibition, and the Depression by keeping grandpa's cautions in mind.

Most Hill residents consistently voted for Democratic Party candidates during the twentieth century. The current Democratic alderman, **Joe Vollmer**, has been in place for seventeen years, and political stability reigned before he won the post. **Robert Ruggeri** was an alderman from 1981 to 1999. He was known for his hard work, networking, incisive debate skills, and loyalty to his constituency. Robert Ruggeri Place in the new La Collina housing development bears his name. **Louis "Midge" Berra**, after whom Berra Park is named, passed in 1964. He rose to become the 24th Ward committeeman, a trusted advisor to St. Louis mayors, the revenue collector, and political patriarch of The Hill.

PROHIBITION AND THE DEPRESSION

Between 1920 and 1940, The Hill experienced its apex of Italian culture and community while at the same time navigating foreboding external and internal forces resulting in a future period of decline and stagnation. Perhaps the apex carried the neighborhood along well enough that it found its footing so as not to fall on its nose.

During the 1920s, The Hill experienced its devotional pinnacle. The donations residents had made finally bore fruit in 1926 with the first mass in the church that literally belonged to the community. Religious festivals flourished and celebrated the feast days of **San Sebastiano**, **Santa Rosalia**, **Our Lady of Mount Carmel**, **St. Dominic**, **St. Joseph**, and the **Feast of Corpus Christi**. A dedicated mass concluded with a processional route that began at the church, wound through The Hill from Marconi to Pattison, south on Edwards, east on Botanical, and back to the church on Marconi. Men carried a statue and were followed by a parade of parishioners stopping at four altars along the corners of the route where priests conducted prayers of thanks supported by the congregation. Those watching the procession from their porches shouted "Viva . . . ," invoking the saint's name and giving a donation. A community picnic with music and dancing followed.

The Hill was enriched by city-funded improvements as well. Perhaps the most significant

Women who worked at Liggett and Myers

A church feast day celebration

Blue Ridge owners
Isidore Oldani and
Louis Venegoni

Leonard, Martin, Louis, and Albert Spielberg

were paved streets, which alleviated the challenges posed by dirt avenues in the summer and mud troughs in the winter. Sewers, gas, and electricity became available and affordable. Jobs were plentiful, as glass and stone businesses flourished in tandem with the iron and steel factories such as **Quick Meal Stove Company**, **McQuay Norris,** and **Carondelet Foundry.** More women worked outside of the home than in previous decades. They worked at factories such as the **Liggett and Myers** tobacco factory, took on piece work at businesses like **Lungstras Cleaners**, or worked at a neighborhood shop or grocery.

Local businesses built by Hill entrepreneurs had become thriving enterprises by the 1920s. **Riggio Realty** formed in 1906, **John Volpi and Company** in 1907, **Sala's** restaurant in 1908, **Ravarino and Freschi Spaghetti** in 1914, **Blue Ridge Bottling** in 1914, **Southwest Bank** in 1920, **Fair Mercantile** in 1920,

The women of Marlo Coil

Spielberg Furniture in 1921, **Missouri Baking Company** in 1924, **Berra Furniture** in 1926, and **St. Louis Macaroni Manufacturing Company** in 1926. Skilled craftsmen contributed to The Hill's growth and character as well. General contractors, carpenters, stone masons, plasterers, and blacksmiths founded family businesses that would last for generations and leave their signature on homes into the 21st century. Barbers, seamstresses, and even certified professional midwives made a living within the neighborhood. The community remained focused on the local, as everything they needed was on The Hill.

The effects of Prohibition, brought on by the 18th Amendment's ratification in 1919, disrupted The Hill's cultural rhythms in two distinct areas: wine and crime. Historic wine-making customs and millennia-old traditions could not be broken in a few years. Hill residents continued to harvest their backyard grape vines to make wine and vinegar for familial consumption. While some local families—those with easy access to sugar or with the ability to create sub-basements two and sometimes three layers deep—did participate wholeheartedly in illegal production and distribution of alcohol, most did not. Many adults on The Hill knew where to find extra wine or alcohol, but they kept quiet. The police resorted to "smelling patrols" where they drove around the neighborhood using proven yet imprecise olfactory detective methods. Once the police discovered a still, they would smash it and the barrels or bottles containing the liquid profits it produced. Local tales still delight the innocent about one big raid in which the fire department came with its pump truck to siphon the illegal hooch into street gutters to run into sewer drains. Local fauna of the two- and four-legged variety imbibed. It was a spectacle.

Pent-up demand for alcohol during Prohibition skewed supply chains, which came under organized gang control stretching from Europe to Cuba, through New York and Chicago, and into

Midwestern cities like St. Louis and Kansas City. Organized criminal elements engaged in the illegal distribution of alcohol and compounded their activities with gambling and protection rackets. While there were turf wars and retribution involving public shootings, arson, and extortion, these events were not the norm usually occurred when outsiders came to the area to make trouble. There is an equal number of stories involving shop owners throwing out immoral customers who tried to do business in their establishment, or business owners returning to Italy to avoid paying protection money. Continuous acts of resistance prevented the neighborhood from becoming a central hub of organized crime. Unfortunately, The Hill gained an unfounded reputation as being a den for the Mafia and as a result endured stereotyping and discrimination for decades.

Missouri Terrazzo Co.

Credit: St. Louis Terrazzo

Missouri Terrazzo Co. opened in 1932 in St. Louis's Fountain Park neighborhood. The company designs and constructs patterned floors using marble and granite terrazzo. It is the only flooring company of its kind in the Midwest. Terrazzo-style flooring originated in Venice, Italy. Pieces of raw material such as granite, quartz, glass, and marble are bound with a cement or epoxy and formed into tile pieces. Generally used on high-traffic floors, the material can also be found on walls and countertops. The possibilities are endless in terms of color, design, and use in mosaics.

Missouri Terrazzo–designed flooring enriches St. Louis Lambert International Airport, the Gateway Arch Museum, and universities and hospitals across the region.

Paul Berra bought the flooring company in 2018 and moved the production facility and offices to The Hill. He intends to grow the enterprise in quality and quantity, thus adding another successful locally owned business to The Hill.

Gaetano Diliberto in his backyard

Just as Prohibition did not alter The Hill's essential character, the Depression did not devastate The Hill's economy or profoundly impact its way of life. Indeed, the immigrant experience had already prepared them for the hardships of the 1930s. The federal government promoted backyard gardens, encouraging Americans to use their yards to grow food. The Hill neighborhood had been practicing local food cultivation since 1900. They raised chickens, rabbits, goats, and even cows. They grew grapes, fruit trees and vines, and vegetables, preserving what they could or bartering their excess for items they could not grow. Only 25 years earlier, they had used the cooperative next to Big Club Hall to share foodstuffs. When heads of household lost their jobs, they sought relief from the mutual aid societies organized by St. Ambrose Church. St. Ambrose Young Men's Sodality, Lady of Mount Carmel (Young Christian Mothers),

Mary Help of Christians, St. Ambrose Alumni Association, the Crusader Club, Troop 212 Boy Scouts of America of St. Ambrose Church, and the Grail Club all formed in the 1930s as a means of coping with the effects of the Depression.

As food and mutual aid kept the most severe effects of the Depression at bay on The Hill, education provided opportunities. The 1930 census shows nearly 30 percent of The Hill's population was under 20 years old. Children had been earning wages as early as eight years old, but by 1930 the national effort for a better-educated populace resulted in children completing grade school and, increasingly, high school. Having children remain in school longer took pressure off the labor market and prepared them to take part in the period of prosperity that began when World War II ended fifteen years later.

THE HILL'S VETERANS

Members of any military branch find support and camaraderie at the Rollo-Calcaterra American Legion Post 15. American World War I veterans of Italian descent formed the Italian American Alliance, which merged with the American Legion in 1926, forming Rollo Post 15, and was expanded after World War II to Rollo-Calcaterra Post 15. The Legion Hall continues to welcome those who served in the military. The post has engaged with the larger Hill community since its inception through sponsorship of post–World War II baseball teams, the annual Easter egg hunt at Berra Park, two annual barbeques, and fish fries during Lent. Post 15 members are an invaluable part of The Hill's veteran and civilian community.

Men and women from The Hill served in every global conflict of the 20th century. World Wars I and II proved difficult since Italy sided against the US for a period during both conflicts.

However, there was no doubt once Italy declared war on the United States: men from The Hill enlisted to serve and defend their country. The names of those lost during World War II are listed on a plaque in the St. Ambrose Church vestibule.

Credits: Barbara Northcott

CUSTOMS AND TRADITIONS

Vibrant communities create a space for members to participate in public celebrations in order to generate a sense of belonging. Centuries of traditional Catholic Church feast days in Europe served to promote well-being and loyalty to church and village. Planning, preparing, executing, and finishing a celebration distributes talents thereby making each villager necessary. This tradition can be seen in The Hill's past and continues today.

FIRE HYDRANTS, COLUMNS, BANNERS, AND SIGNS

According the official website of the city of St. Louis, there are 79 distinct neighborhoods in the city. Many neighborhood associations use branding to denote the character of their districts. The Hill acknowledges its heritage using the colors of the Italian flag. Plucky green, white, and red fire hydrants dot the entire community. The Hill 2000 Neighborhood Association repaints them every few years, in keeping with the tradition of tidiness The Hill is known for. The association quickly sold out of t-shirts they designed that featured a Hill fire hydrant and nothing else—talk about a conversation starter!

Light poles with metal Hill logos indicate The Hill as a destination while providing interesting photographic opportunities. The Hill Business Association initiated the program as well as a map handout indicating Hill businesses and points of interest.

Greek-inspired columns adorn two of the main vehicular entry points into The Hill. Each column marks the boundary with a Hill logo. One of the columns was donated by the Quik-Trip Corporation and placed at the corner of Hampton and Columbia. Another column, funded by a community development grant, stands at the top of The Hill on "the wedge," a boundary indicator where Columbia merges with Southwest and The Hill reaches to the east. The Hill's only water fountain quenches thirst at Berra Park. It could not outrun the painter's brush.

Credit: Barbara Northcott

Credits: Jill Halpin

WEDDINGS

From approximately the 1920s to the late 1980s, weddings on The Hill followed a standard sequence. In the weeks before the wedding, the bride's dress was purchased or sewn. The engaged couple visited the parish priest to make wedding arrangements and discuss their personal and spiritual readiness for the marriage sacrament. Father knew the couple and probably their parents as well. The rehearsal took place in the church and was followed by a meal for both families and the priest.

Weddings became a neighborhood event. Even those who did not know the families personally would go to the church after the mass to watch the grand exit on the church steps. The bride's white, flowing dress contrasted with her new husband's black tuxedo, and the timely pastel of the bridesmaids' gowns added dots of color. Congratulatory wishes barely rose above the excited chatter. When the betrothed came from families with long ties to the neighborhood, a sense of satisfaction reigned with the confidence that the newlyweds would be happy,

have children, and stay on The Hill to continue strengthening our community.

In the past, most Catholic weddings took place on Saturday late morning. A four-hour interval between the wedding and reception allowed time for wedding photos. In St. Louis, couples often took the short drive to the Jewel Box in Forest Park, an arboretum built in 1936 and still brimming with vivid, exotic foliage, guaranteed to match any bridal party's color palate. After photographs, the bridal party spent an hour at a relative's home to refresh and prepare for the evening's upcoming reception festivities.

Puricelli family in 1946 at a wedding reception at Big Club Hall

Wedding party at the Jewel Box in Forest Park

ST. JOSEPH ALTAR

The St. Joseph festival is a millennia-old tradition emanating from Sicily, where St. Joseph is considered a patron saint. It is a springtime celebration thanking the saint for delivering Sicily from drought and famine. Families construct altars in their homes with symbols of gratitude, thus fulfilling the promise to honor St. Joseph for his intervention in ending the hunger. They cover tiered altars with fruits, baked treats, bread, and especially fava beans. Meat offerings are rare because St. Joseph's Day (March 19) occurs during Lent, a time when Catholics forego meat.

The home altars also typically include photos of deceased family members as well as symbols of religious devotion, such as a statue depicting St. Joseph or Mary and Jesus, prayer cards, or white lilies. Dried fava beans are offered because it is said that carrying a fava bean in your wallet ensures you will never go hungry. Families make a full day of visiting friends and relatives who have created altars in their homes.

St. Ambrose Church and School became the central "home" for the St. Joseph Altar. After the 11 a.m. mass in Italian, a procession led by the priest and a devout church member carrying Joseph's statue makes its way to the school cafeteria and gymnasium to be placed on the altar.

The St. Joseph Altar celebration requires a team of organizers and over a year of preparation. Three teams of two people represent the apprentices, the heads, and the advisers, with each team rotating on then off after fulfilling a three-year commitment. The parish's St. Joseph Altar involves the entire community. The event now raises funds through donations, and the money is given to St. Ambrose School for tuition assistance. Parish men and women, along with Hill restaurateurs and food purveyors, donate their considerable skills, energy, and products. Volunteers bring the event together through serving and assisting the hundreds of guests participating in the annual holy day.

Opposite page: The cutwork, or lace, on the St. Joseph Altar cloths were handmade by the women of The Hill.

Procession in Cuggiono, Italy

CORPUS CHRISTI

The eighth Thursday after the Roman Catholic Easter is Corpus Christi, a holy day celebrating the Body of Christ and the gift given through His sacrifice to His followers. St. Ambrose celebrates Corpus Christi by mirroring European traditions of Sunday mass followed by a procession through the community, stopping for prayer at four altars specially constructed for the occasion.

FESTIVALS

Along with community organizations, Hill residents engage in a variety of charitable activities. Annual organized events serve as fundraisers to support their initiatives. While supported by Hill businesses through advertising and sponsorship, metropolitan-wide attendance ensures the events are successful. As with any event on The Hill, volunteers are the principal component. As organizers, workers, and support, they are the essential element to all The Hill's festivals.

GIRO DELLA MONTAGNA

The first Giro della Montagna in 1986 was organized by a team of cycling enthusiasts led by lifelong Hill resident Joe Torrisi. It was a competitive event attracting US Cycling Federation members. After seven years, the Giro became the cornerstone of the newly organized annual Gateway Cup. Decades later, the parent event has changed dates, locations, sponsors, and organizers. It moved from July 4 as part of St. Louis's Independence Day celebrations to Labor Day weekend as the Gateway Cup. There are four participating neighborhoods in the city of St. Louis, each of which hosts a race on one day of the holiday weekend. The Hill continues the cycling tradition on Labor Day Sunday.

The race on The Hill is a criterium or circular route that traverses twelve narrow city blocks with the four corners posing challenging 90-degree turns. Imagine seventy professional cyclists knee-to-knee and wheel-to-wheel, navigating the sharp turns at breakneck speed. The street accommodates three cars side by side, demonstrating how little room there is for racers to take an outside lead. The Hill is indeed on a hill, requiring cyclists to race up a steep slope and navigate a perilous descent, judiciously balancing speed and position. Watching the pro teams execute strategy and yet remain adaptive impresses cycling aficionados.

The Hill residents in the interior of the racecourse make the day a celebration. They set up canopies in the streets to watch the races and have a block party during the daylong event, with barbeque, coolers, music, yard games, and open houses. Volunteers for the event also drive its success. They set up the viewers' grandstand on the church stairs and staff booths selling Italian favorites such as salsiccia sandwiches, toasted ravioli, spedini, and cannoli. Above all, the cyclists enjoy the challenging course and appreciate the old-world hospitality.

WINE WALK

The Italian American Chamber of Commerce along with The Hill Business Association initiated the first Hill Wine Walk. Since 2011, Hill businesses have offered a hospitable welcome to visitors seeking good wine, Italian nibbles, and unique specialty items from Hill shops. Two dozen businesses open their doors to the curious and enthusiastic. Once Wine Walkers check in to receive their commemorative cup, wrist band, and map, they're ready to explore The Hill and discover its enigmatic treasures. They might find anything from a camera obscura in a soap shop to a live band in a back room, but they will surely find interesting wines and tasty treats. The Wine Walk raises funds for The Hill Business Association's marketing and collaboration efforts.

Hill Lore

Joe DeGregorio continues in his father's footsteps in The Hill tour business. Roland DeGregorio was a mailman on The Hill for decades. After retiring, Joe stepped into his father's shoes, providing hundreds of people with colorful history and insights into Hill lore. In 2019, Joe received an award from the Italian Club honoring him for his work in promoting Italian culture.

HILL DAY

Hill Day was a neighborhood celebration of our Italian immigrant past. The first event was in 1965 as part of a citywide 200-year anniversary celebration acknowledging St. Louis's distinct ethnic neighborhoods. Father Salvatore Polizzi was the driving force behind Hill Day. Through his exemplary leadership, he ensured that The Hill would be prominently featured in the year-long festivities. He organized the 21 committees of the first Hill Day to accommodate thousands of guests to the neighborhood. The neighborhood's efforts were so successful, Hill Day continued as a fundraiser for the community for years to come. The festival featured a parade with handmade floats honoring Italy's famous landmarks such as the leaning tower of Pisa and the Colosseum. Plentiful Italian food stalls served traditional grilled salciccia or saucy meatball sandwiches among other Italian favorites. At the craft fair, neighborhood women proudly displayed handmade tablecloths embellished with cutwork, dolls dressed in handmade ball gowns, pinwheel yard flowers, and quilts and crochet—lots of crochet. The women donated material and expertise, crafting all year to raise funds for the community. Traditional songs inspired practiced dancers who performed on the St. Ambrose Church steps, also known as the stage and dais. Food and fun were served Italian style, complemented by an orchestra, grape stomping, and spaghetti-eating contests. Visitors can still spot the traditional metal beer bucket with "Hill Day" emblazoned over a green, white, and red flag holding pens in a shop or on the collectible shelf in a home. Hill Day grew into a trendy affair welcoming hundreds of thousands of people over the years.

Preparation for the next Hill Day began more than a year in advance. Three co-chairs managed the event logistics. One

was the primary chair from the previous year, one was the current primary chair, and one would be the chair next year. The triad shared the planning and management responsibilities while delivering a consistent product. They were assisted by a St. Ambrose priest who oversaw the church's parking lot and lower level as well as the grade school's facilities, all of which were used by Hill Day committees. In addition to the priest and co-chairs, 21 committees conducted the planning and execution

of Hill Day. Several hundred Hill residents gave thousands of hours of volunteer time and donated money to ensure a well-organized, successful event. Hill Day has taken on an almost mythical status. Recently, one St. Louis reporter remembered his youthful years at Hill Days, and upon seeing an antique beer bucket had to find a measuring cup to see exactly how much beer it held. There was a story there, but he wasn't sharing! His experience was not unique.

In 1975, Hill Day organizers took a break to prepare for the nation's bicentennial celebrations in the coming year. Celebrating the United States' 200th anniversary enabled Italian immigrants and their families to show their loyalty to their adopted country even as they clung to cultural practices from their ancestral home. By the last Hill Day in 1979, the crowds overwhelmed the small neighborhood, which could no longer bear the damage done by revelers to property and spirit. But the harm was superficial and the fatigue temporary. While Hill Day itself is no longer celebrated, the neighborhood still welcomes visitors to enjoy festivals that are smaller in size yet greater in number.

Italian Songs

 The Hill Day organizers produced a vinyl record album of traditional Italian songs and sold it as a fundraiser at the 1973 Hill Day.

LA FESTA

The festival, or La Festa, is a street festival organized by committees associated with St. Ambrose. It serves two purposes: raising money for the school and church but also bringing back a smaller, local version of Hill Day. The traditional Italian Band plays on the church steps while familiar activities ranging from a cake walk to quilt raffles to assorted games of chance and skill provide a long afternoon of entertainment. Naturally, barbequed salciccia and cold beer are the staples of sustenance. Toasted ravioli, cannoli, and brick-fired pizza joined salciccia sandwiches as culinary mainstays. Wine, mixed drinks, slushies, and hand-squeezed lemonade broaden the beverage menu. While the traditional band plays, carnival rides, bouncy houses, and even a climbing wall round out the fun. It is a familiar annual gathering where long tables with chairs welcome longtime friends and extended families who have gathered for an informal reunion.

ITALIAN HERITAGE PARADE AND FESTA

Columbus Day was declared a federal holiday in 1971 on the second Monday in October to coincide with October 10, the traditional memorial day. Previously, the city of St. Louis had passed an ordinance in 1919 for the Genoan navigator.

The legacy of Christopher Columbus winds through St. Louis history like the parades in his honor wound through the city's streets. Just as public perception of his impact on the Americas has waxed and waned, so too have the composition and volume of the celebrations recognizing him.

The Fratellanza Society staged the first Columbus Day celebration in St. Louis in 1867. Initially, the parade traversed through parts of downtown and included notable Italian Americans walking or riding horses. A brass band accompanied men and women in full regalia depicting various regions in Italy and showcasing traditional dance. Later, the Knights of Columbus took responsibility for the annual celebration.

In 1979, The Hill 2000 community organization moved the parade home where the route began in front of Southwest Bank at Kingshighway and Southwest and then went west to Marconi northward, where it passed in front of St. Ambrose Church before concluding at Berra Park at Shaw and Macklind for the Festa. While separate organizations took turns coordinating the parade and festivities, it remained a continuous annual event.

In 1992, the parade and festivities were organized by the St. Louis Columbus Day Corporation, an umbrella organization encompassing various groups interested in preserving Italian heritage. Hill parade organizers made contributions to the event, including vintage cars carrying priests, bishops, nuns, local political candidates, and top elected officials such as the mayor of St. Louis and senators and representatives; a thirty-foot-long Italian Special sandwich; a twenty-foot-high (motorized) shopping cart from a hometown grocer; and a vintage fire truck owned and driven by a local merchant. Police records estimate that 5,000 people lined the parade route that was less than a mile long. Spectators moved to Berra Park, where the Italian Band played on the stage, food booths enticed attendees with Italian treats, games engaged children and adults, and the picnic atmosphere extended into the evening. Perhaps as a result of a lifetime of conditioning, upon hearing the 6 p.m. church bells, Hill residents packed up to go home, though not before picking up a bit of trash and folding a chair or two before they left. Today, we celebrate our immigrant ancestors with the Italian Heritage Parade and Festa.

TURKEY BOWL

In 1928, Hill residents enjoyed the first Turkey Bowl Thanksgiving Day soccer tournament. Members of The Hill's athletic clubs faced off in two teams, the "ol-timers" and the "youngsters." Since 1928, the designation of who is a youngster and who is an ol-timer still hasn't been fully resolved. Because it is an open community event, any male (and more recently, any female) with known talent can play. The players are split into even teams of young and old, depending on who shows up. Looking at past accounts of the event, it seems the win/loss records are divided. Sometimes experience wins over speed, and sometimes it's the opposite.

The soccer game is a fundraiser that regularly raises over $1,000 for the St. Vincent de Paul Society, which clothes, feeds, and shelters the poor. Most of the neighborhood moseys to the park during the game. The alderman for The Hill and owner of Milo's Bocce Garden donates and cooks luganiga (mild Italian sausage) sandwiches, while the Missouri Baking Company provides pastries and coffee, as they have done for decades. Hill residents come to the event to watch the game and to socialize,

regardless of the weather. Even as spectators catch up on the news, they always keep an eye on the field. They know the guys playing are exceptional soccer players because they are college All-Americans, professional indoor and outdoor players, and in years gone by members of the US World Cup team. They represent a continuity of Hill legacy.

The pregame at the bowl pits the seventh graders against the eighth graders. Some of these players will become Turkey Bowl regulars.

ANNUAL SOAP BOX DERBY AND CUSTOM CAR SHOW

There isn't anything specifically Italian about a soap box derby. Nevertheless, it is an event The Hill community has embraced since 1977. The Hill hosts the only St. Louis derby where racers qualify to go to the national competition in Dayton, Ohio. The annual race on The Hill takes place during the weekend before Father's Day in June.

In partnership with the St. Louis Jaycees, who organize and officiate the race, Hill businesses sponsor the event and Hill volunteers work it. Any boy or girl from 7 to 18 can apply to be included in the lineup. All racers use the officially sanctioned derby car kit, which ranges from $390 to $850. Racers are encouraged to secure a sponsor who will pay for the kit as an advertisement and donation. Additionally, all racers must work with an adult from beginning to end to secure funding, assemble the car kit, and attend the race. The program intentionally seeks to build self-reliance and confidence and to encourage a closer child-mentor relationship. Young racers develop an appreciation of craftsmanship and the work required to complete the project.

When drivers careen down Macklind Avenue at top speeds of 30 mph, they are reminded that they indeed live on a hill. As the race has progressed over the years, neither boys nor girls have dominated the winner's circle. The same is true for the derby's special guests. Traditionally, the fire chief and police chief of the city of St. Louis compete. While each has earned bragging rights over the years, the fire chief seems to have a couple more wins under his belt. This might be due to his skill or to his experience (since he's been at the wheel longer). He enjoys taking home the coveted Oil Can Trophy.

During the races, the sizeable Shaw School parking lot hosts over 100 custom antique cars, sponsored by Hill businesses **Southwest Auto Parts** and **Auto Art**. The cars range from restored roadrunners to mint-condition classics. The casual party mood surrounds car owners and enthusiasts engaged in lively conversations about restoration or epic road trips in their rebuilt dynamos. The derby and car show complement each other by allowing both children and adults to learn and demonstrate hard work, determination, camaraderie, and the value of friendly competition.

Fire chief at the derby

CHRISTMAS ON THE HILL

Every December, The Hill businesses and organizations offer an open invitation to celebrate the holiday season on The Hill. Festivities feature Santa Claus and his Italian counterpart, La Befana, along with carriage rides, roasted chestnuts, and holiday markets featuring baked goods and handcrafted items from the Sacred Heart Villa and knitted, crocheted, and handmade gifts from the Lower Level Ladies. The Hill vendors sell special treats while Hill organizations offer a petting zoo, face painting, cookie decorating, and lots of hot chocolate. Throughout December, Hill vendors also host a nativity walk showcasing nativity scenes from Italy.

THE HILL 2000
A NEIGHBORHOOD ASSOCIATION

DECEMBER 2014 · VOLUME 45 · ISSUE 12

Merry Christmas
Buon Natale

Celebrate The Hill this Holiday Season!

December 6
CHRISTMAS ON THE HILL

12:00	**Walking Tour of The Hill**
	St. Ambrose Church
1:00	**La Befana**
	Gelató di Riso
	Walking Tour of The Hill
	St. Ambrose Church
1:00 - 7:00	**Carriage Rides**
	Girasole
1:00 - ?	**Salsiccia**
	Church Yard
2:00	**La Befana**
	Girasole
	Walking Tour of The Hill
	St. Ambrose Church

Cartoon of the Festa by Frank "Chick" Severino

The Hill 2000 Neighborhood Association and
The Hill Business Association Proudly Presents

THE HILL

House Tour
Yesterday, Today and Tomorrow

Sunday June 24, 2018
| 1:00 ~ 5:00 pm | Tickets $20.00 |

Purchase Tickets at the Hill Neighborhood Center
Call 1-314-260-9162 or www.hillstl.org

HILL HOUSE TOUR

Hill Neighborhood Center volunteers organized the first Hill House Tour in 2018. On a June afternoon, private homeowners welcomed four hundred ticket-holders to see residences—representing construction styles ranging from shotgun to bungalow to newer construction—that have been renovated, updated, improved, and custom-built to meet the needs of today's families.

The Hill has dozens of homes built more than 100 years ago in sturdy brick, many of which are still in remarkable condition. Even though these houses have a small footprint, their designers imagined unique ways to add living space. For example, by building a loft in the attic, one homeowner managed to convert previously unused space into a private office. Several other homes on display revealed imaginative floor plans and repurposed areas. A Murphy bed in a main living room proved a practical alternative to dedicating a room to just one use. Other homeowners built entire second floors on top of existing buildings. Truly, the sky is the limit.

A second Hill House Tour in 2019 proved equally successful, with a new slate of homes for viewing and more tickets sold. The success of the house tours is attributed to hard-working volunteers and generous homeowners.

Through the growing diversity of architectural styles, the streets remain clean and neat, and the sidewalks are clear of low branches, vegetation, and house boundary encroachments. In the past, The Hill was described as a neighborhood characterized by neat rows of houses. That's still true today, as The Hill remains a desirable place to live and one worth the investment.

BIG CLUB HALL

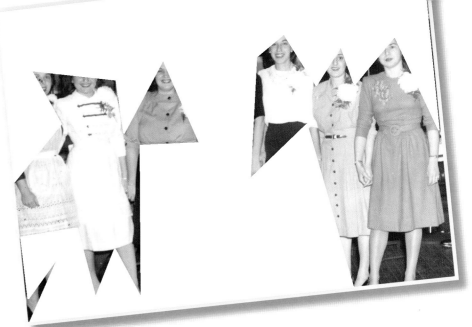

Grail event at Big Club Hall

Any Hill resident born before 1964 remembers a wedding reception at Big Club Hall. The women in charge of the food began cooking the day before the reception. They made ravioli from scratch, prepared chicken for roasting, and cooked beef for slicing. The wedding meal started with a salad lightly dressed in seasoned oil and vinegar along with plates of salami, ham, mortadella, and cheese and rolls. The servers placed the food on long tables, family style, with expert precision. They brought ravioli in a light tomato sauce, followed by roasted chicken with a deliciously tacky thin skin coating that frustrated many a home cook who tried to replicate it. The meal ended with sliced beef in light gravy and another Italian bun. Dessert was either a piece of wedding cake, Italian cookies, or spumoni. Women often tucked wrapped wedding cake in their purse to be enjoyed with breakfast the following morning. Everyone experienced a Big Club Hall wedding one way or another. The youngsters waited outside while one of their mates snuck up the grand stairs to the reception

hall to ask for a beef sandwich. His bravery was rewarded with delicious treats for him and his pals. They danced inside and out to the live band playing traditional Italian music mixed in with contemporary tunes.

Today, it is hard for any Hill resident to walk by the Big Club Hall building and not smile at the fond memories wafting out of the building like Italian epicurean delights dancing on an Italian song. Residents are grateful that the building remains and that the digital/visual artist who owns it takes exceptional care of it.

PALMA AUGUSTA

la riunione

The Palma Augusta at 1920 Marconi was the Sicilian response to Big Club Hall and was located right across the street from it. The one-story structure served the Sicilian community on The Hill, just as Big Club Hall served the Lombards, especially during the pre–World War II years.

The regional segregation between the two venues was fluid at best. Sicilian families used the larger Big Club Hall just as Lombards used the cozier and less expensive Palma Augusta. Wedding receptions at both were a regular occurrence.

The Palma Augusta served as a meeting house for anti-fascists in the area. They invited anti-Hitler and anti-Mussolini speakers from as far away as Chicago to speak about the plight of Italy's ordinary citizens under fascism. They rallied Italian Americans to push back against Mussolini's sympathizers in the United States.

Today, the building is subdivided into three business fronts.

ORGANIZATIONS

The structure of The Hill is often described as three-legged—St. Ambrose Church (spiritual), The Hill 2000 Neighborhood Association (civic), and The Hill Business Association (commerce). They work together, along with the City of St. Louis alderman, to ensure the stability and well-being of the neighborhood. It must be noted that each of these legs benefits from additional supports such as the charitable good works of the St. Ambrose Society and the community-minded Block Captain program.

The Wildcats

Hawks baseball

CLUBS AND CAUSINO

Visitors to The Hill observe that our generations-old community is tight knit. A primary contributor to our cohesiveness is St. Ambrose, the center of our spiritual community. In addition, family relations can be traced back four or five generations, including direct relations, marriages, and adopted kin. Houses and businesses often stay in the family, creating anchors that hold the community steady as St. Louis experiences political and civic changes.

Another type of bond formed among the boys and young men of The Hill. Between the 1930s and early 1970s, houses were small and families large, and children didn't want to be confined to the house. They did not have hours of homework to do as our children do today, and during the early years there was no television. They played games outside in the streets—not in the yards, which were small and occupied with vegetable gardens for family meals. The row of houses on either side and the cross street at either end of the block were natural barriers. Children

did not stray far from their home block. Parents either sat on the porch or peeked outside regularly to supervise. The kids knew to be home when the church bells rang, a factory whistle blew, or later when the streetlights came on.

To occupy themselves, the boys turned to sports. They organized teams with one end of the block competing against the other in soccer, baseball, corkball, and street hockey. They improvised using old magazines for shin guards, balls of tape for a baseball, or hand-me-down baseball gloves padded with

old newspapers. Their ingenuity was impressive. Eventually the teams formed clubs in order to widen the competition beyond the kids at the other end of the block. They mirrored their fathers' clubs by giving themselves a name, securing a clubhouse, charging membership, and holding weekly meetings complete with elected officers.

Joe Causino of the Southside YMCA deserves credit for organizing over 2,000 young men into clubs. He embodied the solution to a nationwide burgeoning juvenile delinquency crisis in the fifteen years before World War II. He taught the boys

how to create and maintain a club, and he modeled personal responsibility, community stewardship, and leadership skills. He taught the boys how to secure their clubhouses and furnish them with second-hand materials like old ping-pong tables, phonographs, horseshoe sets, used musical instruments, and sports gear. He coached them on how to court sponsors who paid for their club uniforms, thus advertising at the intramural club tournaments and league games.

Over 30 clubs formed on The Hill between the 1930s and 1970s. Most boys joined at eight or nine years old and identified with the club for their entire life. They will always be a Fawn, Wild Cat, Pelican, Hawk, HIP, Viking, Crusader, Raven, Stag, Hill Topper, Gloom Chaser, or Royal Falcon. Their clubhouse and field of choice defined them and instilled pride. They invited their sponsors, families, and friends to their open houses so they could show off their digs. They took pride in having a clean, orderly clubhouse, to the point of charging a fine to any boy who damaged furniture. If a conflict erupted, the members tried to resolve it internally; if that wasn't possible, they called on Mr. Causino. Each club had a unique character. Some excelled in soccer, baseball, or softball; some left legacies such as a community newspaper or fundraisers for returning World War II soldiers; and some were great dancers, musicians, or stage actors.

In the mid-1980s organizers staged a reunion for all The Hill clubs. They rented the largest event hall in the area that could comfortably hold 600 people. Tickets for the dinner dance sold out quickly—but that didn't stop another 200 from crashing the party! Though the fire chief might not have approved, the guests rejoiced in the noisy celebration of lifelong friends. After all, they grew up on The Hill, so a crowded dinner table was normal.

The club paradigm lives on in the Crusaders, now a legacy organization, and The Hill Boys, who are getting close to retirement. The Hill Boys collectively earned the Italian American Heritage Award in 2020 for their charitable contributions and for hundreds of hours of labor given to Hill projects and events.

PROFESSIONAL AND BUSINESS CLUBS

The **Professional and Business Men's Club of The Hill** formed in 1949. Known as "the helping hand of The Hill," the club provided college scholarships to students from The Hill who might not otherwise have been able to afford to further their education. Over the years, the club members raised hundreds of thousands of dollars.

The 200-plus-member PBM did not have a formal clubhouse or headquarters, though they met monthly at Ruggeri's Restaurant for a meal and a meeting, with emphasis on the meal. Though they were an informal organization, they managed the funding and allocation of well over 100 scholarships. In 1974, their eighteenth year of giving, they finally selected five young women to receive the scholarship because members realized that higher education opportunities had opened to women, who were also children of The Hill.

In 1984, the **Business and Professional Women's Club of The Hill** was formed. Its goal was to empower the women of

The Hill personally, politically, and professionally through national conventions and business association sessions at the chapter level. The organization provided a space for professional women to network and learn how to succeed in a competitive business environment.

HILL 2000 NEIGHBORHOOD ASSOCIATION

Densely populated urban areas across the United States experienced a divergent set of challenges in the 1960s and 1970s. The millions of post–World War II babies were growing up and looking for houses of their own. Because cars (new and used) had become available and postwar highway development enabled workers to commute to the city for work while living in the outlying areas, the urban landscape began to decay. There was little tax base to pay for the repairs and maintenance needed in older cities, and once an area becomes weakened, it can enter a death spiral. Once proud and storied St. Louis city neighborhoods crumbled.

The Hill experienced these same forces. Fortunately, prescient neighborhood leaders understood the threat and sought to protect The Hill's identity as a desirable place to live. The Improvement Association of The Hill formed in 1964. In 1965, believing a drive-in theater on Wilson Avenue would damage the residential integrity of their neighborhood, Hill residents blocked the business venture. The residents realized they had the power to protect the neighborhood through focused, organized action.

A national lead company proposed disposing of clay slurry into abandoned mine shafts in the late 1960s. The company had recently been prohibited from draining water and ore waste into the River des Peres because the city's treatment plant could no longer remediate the waste. The mineral company's leadership responded with a plan to pipe wastewater up the riverbank

Hill 2000 Office on Shaw Avenue, 1970s

into the abandoned mine shafts in Berra Park. In response, a neighborhood group presented a petition with 1,300 signatures opposing the initiative. After a long legal battle, The Hill prevailed.

The previous battles turned out to be training for the next campaign. In 1956, the federal highway department announced that the new Interstate 44 would cut through the northern section of The Hill separating more than 100 homes from the rest of the neighborhood and demolishing another 100. The entire length of the south side of Pattison Avenue was slated to be razed. Furthermore, residents on the north side would only have a walking bridge to get to church or any of the local businesses. Cars would have to use Kingshighway on the east or Macklind on the west to get into the neighborhood. At one point, the highway commission even proposed putting an entrance/exit ramp at Macklind and the new I-44, rendering Berra Park useless as a public space.

The Hill leadership, directed most vocally by Assistant Pastor (now Monsignor) Salvatore Polizzi, took concerned citizens by the busload to the state capital in Jefferson City and then took a dozen or so to Washington, DC. Supported by our senators and representatives, they pleaded the neighborhood's case. The neighborhood committee fought the entry/exit ramp successfully. Hampton and Kingshighway became the west and east highway access points, though residents still wanted a bridge over I-44 for cars and a walkway. Through generous donations from business leaders and the community, The Hill negotiating team offered $50,000 to the government to build the bridge, naturally garnering favorable national news coverage. Perhaps aided by the fact that the transportation secretary was named Volpe, The Hill won its overpass.

It was a pyrrhic victory, as there was nothing the community could do to stop the pain and devastation yet to come. The federal government claimed eminent domain and bought the houses for the prices that families had paid for them 40 years earlier. Families were first threatened with immediate eviction, then allowed to stay until the construction machinery moved closer. Those who remained paid rent to their new landlord, the government. Two-thirds of the families found homes on or near The Hill, but one third had to find homes in other neighborhoods. Seniors today still get emotional when they recall being separated from their homes, and more importantly, their families.

Hill 2000 Incorporated formed in 1969 as a result of these battles and inspired by an article in the *St. Louis Post-Dispatch* about the Soulard Neighborhood's residents actively seeking to bring residents back to their community. Its tag line was "Pride Builds," which subtly referenced the immigrant pride of having built a thriving, unified space. The mission became embodied in an office building where volunteers met, coordinated, and planned. They became a clearinghouse connecting house sellers to buyers and employers to workers. They assisted

Senior trip

non–English speakers with official documents and helped residents apply for home-improvement grants. Their monthly newsletter kept the neighborhood informed and created buy-in into Hill 2000 so residents felt they owned a part of the community. Hill 2000 successfully inspired residents to emulate the village sentiment our families left in Italy.

The Hill 2000 organization became a model for neighborhoods across the country that were fighting against urban decay. Father Salvatore Polizzi, a St. Ambrose parish priest, earned his master's degree from Saint Louis University with a focus on revitalizing local communities. His passion for The Hill's legacy and future as an ethnic enclave perseveres.

The Hill 2000 Senior Citizens program flourished from the 1950s through the 1980s. The program's members met weekly to enjoy lunch, play shuffleboard, and plan trips all across the country. They traveled by bus to cities such as Memphis, Denver, and Milwaukee and took occasional day trips around the region. Their enthusiastic camaraderie recalled the days when they went to school or church as adolescents!

Today, The Hill 2000 Neighborhood Association still has a nine-member board elected by association members. It holds a neighborhood meeting every other month and a monthly board meeting. The board members continue to respond to the community's needs. In 2018, Hill 2000 subsidized video doorbells. The program enabled neighbors to share recorded incidents with each other and with the police. A monthly neighborhood newsletter with full-color photos delights members, and they get very upset if they miss an issue! Annual events such as the Easter egg hunt, Hill House Tours, Giro della Montagna, the Italian Heritage Day Parade, and Festa/Christmas on The Hill serve as fundraisers for general operations including The Hill Neighborhood Center.

Orchids and Onions

Credit: Jill Halpin

THE HILL NEIGHBORHOOD CENTER

The Hill 2000 Neighborhood Center on the corner of Marconi and Daggett Avenues replaced the old offices on Shaw Avenue. It welcomes visitors to The Hill and provides them with maps, directions, and information about Hill history as well as current and future events. It is an inviting space where a new visitor or resident can get their bearings and find the many spots on The Hill that pique their interest.

Residents and visitors alike use genealogy services provided by skilled, knowledgeable volunteers who are from families native to The Hill. The Center houses an archive and database containing artifacts and photos donated by Hill friends and families. It is an epicenter of pop culture's six degrees of separation, where people find connections through the most unexpected avenues. For

Frank Borghi and Joe Numi

example, a Hill native's daughter moved out of state and became friends with a peer whose family had roots on The Hill. Eventually, she learned that this friend's great uncle was the doctor who delivered her father! The stories are extraordinary.

To keep the past alive, displays of Hill history hang from the walls, and informative artifacts explain specific aspects of Hill life. Students at all levels are welcome to use the archives for primary source research. Additionally, the Center is a hub during neighborhood special events, hosts cooking demonstrations, and has meeting rooms for hire.

SICK AND ELDERLY PROGRAM OF THE HILL

The Sick and Elderly Program of The Hill was founded by John and RoseMarie Bianchi, and their family continues to serve the elderly in the neighborhood today. They have served over 4,000 people since 1975, and their skillful, compassionate work has earned them the gratitude of generations.

The Sick and Elderly Program's primary fundraiser takes place annually in September. The Ravioli Dinner shows The Hill's community commitment at its best. Volunteers who informally apprenticed for years cook sauce and ravioli and prepare salad. The Hill's oldest bakery supplies dozens of full sheet cakes for dessert, while another bakery donates bread. The grade school children collect trays and keep tables clean. It is an enjoyable meal blessed by families for the well-being of our seniors.

John and RoseMarie Bianchi

THE HILL BUSINESS ASSOCIATION

The Hill Business Association (HBA) formed in 1997 in order to secure City renewal grants to revitalize Hill business building facades. It evolved onto an organization dedicated to meeting the needs of the newest generation of Hill entrepreneurs through networking, collaboration, and mutual support. The organization is housed at The Hill Neighborhood Center. Members must either have a business on The Hill or personally live on The Hill. The organization intends to complement The Hill 2000 Neighborhood Association but with businesspeople as members. They promote individual industry through virtual marketing platforms, and they collaborate on projects promoting Hill ventures.

The organization provides complimentary informational maps for visitors to The Hill. Because of its marketing efforts, The Hill is the second-most requested information according to St. Louis's promotional body, Explore St. Louis.

The HBA hosts the annual Wine Walk, which sells out each year, and supports the Soap Box Derby and Car Show. Information about Hill businesses can be found on the HBA's collaborative website.

ENTERTAINMENT

Continuing millennia-old traditions, The Hill residents love their performance art. They get excited over music old and new, performed live and recorded, instrumental, opera, or *a cappella*. If it's a song, it's gotta be good.

THE HILL'S DIVAS
Toni Carroll

To categorize Toni Carroll as a character would be an understatement! Born Lorraine Iadreschi in Italy in the 1920s, she came with her parents to The Hill when she was eight years old. Naturally talented, she took voice lessons while still in grade school. She also went to Washington University's Kroeger School of Music, which was founded by Ernest Kroeger, master of programs for the Bureau of Music at the St. Louis 1904 World's Fair. When finished, she bolted to New York City searching for opportunities. Toni's first job groomed her for prospects to come. She could sing, had an hourglass figure, and stood five feet seven inches tall—the perfect Copacabana girl. She added chorus girl at the prestigious Latin Quarter nightclub to her portfolio, and she mixed with the talented and famous, such as Jimmy Durante, Frank Sinatra, Mae West, Milton Berle, and the Andrews Sisters.

They inspired her to try cinematic acting, resulting in small movie roles and guest appearances on television programs, though her voice saved her once again. She performed on stage across America, and she recorded several albums for RCA Victor and MGM Records that are

still available for sale. Toni even had an old home week when Joe Garagiola guest hosted for Johnny Carson's *Late Show*. Joe included both Yogi Berra and Toni as guests one night, perhaps with the intention of embarrassing the shy Yankee. Joe almost fell out of his chair laughing as Toni practically sat on Yogi's lap insisting he sing "Volare" with her in Italian! He was a good sport though, and Toni had a great time.

In October 1958, Toni traveled across Europe. As she moved east toward the Soviet Union, the American Embassy in Moscow arranged for an informal performance. She became the first American singer and recording artist to sing at the Moscow Art Theatre. The fans loved her. The message she took to Americans and Russians was a plea for open dialogue instead of Cold War scolding.

Ms. Carroll dabbled in the spirit world, and it worked for her. She was driving her car through Oklahoma's desolate oil fields and happened upon a man fixing his oil drill. After a long conversation, Toni believed she could divine the right location for an oil well. She was super lucky or super right, because she found three successful wells, profiting handsomely. She currently lives comfortably in New York.

Gina Galati

Gina Galati (daughter of Dominic and Jackie Galati of Dominic's Restaurant) is also the founder and general director of Winter Opera St. Louis, now in its 14th season. New Opera performs during the winter months only, leaving the soprano available to perform casual operatic evenings or Opera Nights on The Hill. Dominic's provides the four-course dinner, and Gina assembles the opera talent of two to four singers per evening. The intimate, delicious Opera Nights enthrall admirers from The Hill to the far corners of the globe.

Ms. Galati manages a successful opera company, drawing talent from the United States and beyond. Her company rehearses at their studio on The Hill, ensuring opera has a home in St. Louis.

Her professional debut as Musetta with the Wichita Grand Opera blossomed into roles as the heroine Rosina in *The Barber of Seville*, Mimì and Musetta in *La Bohème*, Nedda in *I Pagliacci*, Donna Elvira in *Don Giovanni*, Norina in *Don Pasquale*, and Gilda in Verdi's *Rigoletto*. Ms. Galati garnered an international following through her performances with operatic companies in Miami; Brooklyn; Naples, Italy; Medellin, Colombia; and Opera Prolirica in South America.

Kathryn Favazza

St. Louisan Kathryn Favazza has been described as having "a lustrous voice and a commanding range that captures her audience." She has performed concerts at Carnegie Hall and has delighted audiences as Adina (*L'Elisir d'Amore*), Gilda (*Rigoletto*), and Lucia (*Lucia di Lammermoor*). Kathryn has performed with the Riverside Opera, the Garden State Opera, and Smithtown Opera, among others. She's also performed in concerts including Handel's Messiah, Fauré's Requiem, the St. John Passion, and St. Matthew Passion with orchestras including the Brooklyn Conservatory and the Garden State Philharmonic, and for many years she has been the featured soloist for the Christmas on The Hill Concert.

Maria Rose

In the 1930s, mezzo-soprano Maria Russo enjoyed enthusiastic support from her immigrant parents. She sang as soon as she could talk. Her silky, strong voice reminded her father of the women of Italy singing through their daily chores. She began taking lessons at 11 years old. Maria's voice carried throughout her family's produce shop so clearly that a salesman visiting the shop could not help but notice. He introduced Maria to a professional voice coach who happened to be his son's mother-in-law. The coach was a fierce taskmaster who worked with Maria until she was ready to take her chances in New York. After graduating from Loretto Academy in St. Louis, she moved to New York to audition and to study under Maestro Giovanni Usellini (aka Renato Cellini). Her mother and brother, an aspiring clarinet player, lived with Maria during the winter season. They would join the family back in St. Louis for the summer.

Maria traveled with operatic companies throughout the United States, Cuba, and Colombia. Her proudest moment was in 1949, when she came back to St. Louis and The Hill for her hometown debut with the 85-piece St. Louis Symphony Orchestra at the Opera House in Kiel Auditorium. Friends and family from The Hill bought over 100 tickets to support one of their own.

Performing the Tarantella, a traditional Italian dance.

ARTS AND ENTERTAINMENT ON THE HILL

The Italians love their song, opera, musical instruments, and theatrical performance. The desire to enjoy life through music and lyrics ranging from pious, to gripping, to funny, and even suggestive is deeply embedded in the idea of what "Italian-ness" means. The Hill community continues to be enriched by Italy's cultural legacy. The waiters at the long-closed Ruggeri's Restaurant impacted their younger counterparts so much that upon answering a phone call from one of these tenors you may be greeted with an *a cappella* serenade! It is still a treat to watch a skilled accordion performance, and while walking down the streets of the neighborhood you may hear drummers practicing or guitar players strumming. You might even hear a ukulele. Small ensembles perform during the summer at Hill restaurants, and bands are ubiquitous at Hill events.

Winter Opera St. Louis, an opera company with an office and practice studio on The Hill, stages productions from November through March.

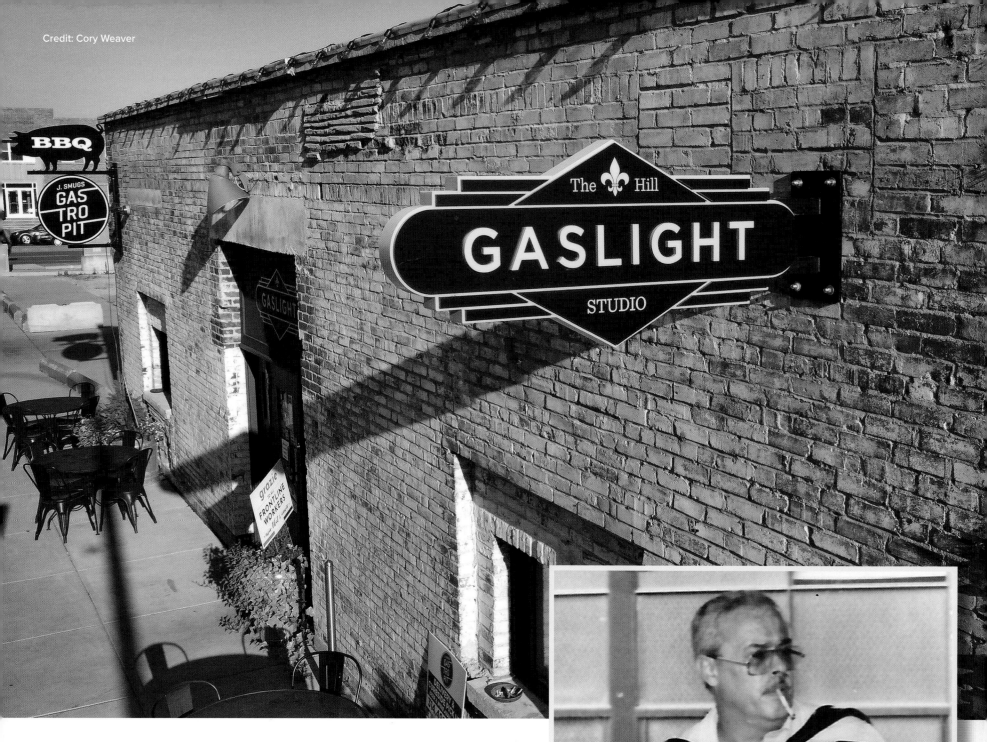

Gaslight Studio offers local talent the chance to entertain and record in their unique tavern/recording studio. While patrons may not hear music made in Italy, the spirit of engaging and supporting musical performers continues.

During the 1960s and 1970s, an assemblage of unequivocally talented performers from The Hill regaled the neighborhood with their uninhibited theatrical productions. They performed mostly in the St. Ambrose Grade School gym to raise money for the school or other neighborhood projects. The gifted troupe wrote the dialogue and the music scores, choreographed dance

Casa e Cucina

Left to right: **Norma Griffero, Gloria Griffero, and Maggie Griffero**

The Merlo family exemplifies fun, talent, and commitment to the community.

Linda Hausman and Ernie Hausman

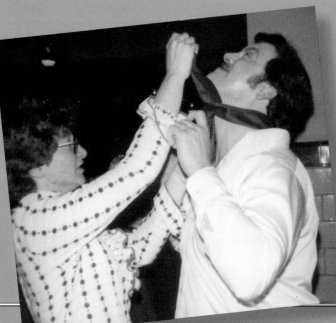

routines and taught dancers, designed and sewed the costumes, built theater sets, and organized logistics from marketing to play programs to set teardown. Carpenters, musicians, seamstresses, young and old, moms, dads, and grandparents lent a hand for the shows. *Apple Fever, Duck, the Garlic's Flying,* and the *Déjà Vu Revue* (I and II) were some of their many successes. It remains a mystery how grown men and women could completely lose their inhibitions. When asked how so many people could work so hard to have a good laugh, one of the organizers known for her perpetual motion said that they did it for fun. And, they did it for the community. "We all knew each other back then and we pooled our talents. Friends and family came to see us and we all had a good time."

The budding thespians of the 1960s were informed by their childhood experiences of neighborhood troupes and venues. **The Vincenzo Bellini Club** offered regular choral recitals and operas in Italian in the 1930s. Informal gatherings in the open fields of the 1910s and 1920s provided a regular picnic opportunity to enjoy local talent—something like an open mic night.

The movie theaters on The Hill—the **Family Theater** and the **Columbia Theater**—offered vaudeville acts, silent movies, and finally talkies. Managed by Hill resident Joe Tapella and owned by Bess Schulter and George Skouras, The Columbia reached across generations in its 50-year life from the 1920s to the 1970s. After a short stint as a private racquetball club, today the building is a private residence and also houses the Columbia Foundation for the Arts.

The nightclubs reached their height in the 1920s, when it was fashionable for young, wealthy St. Louisans to visit **Club Casino** or the **Savoy Garden** during a long night out on the town. While there are no more nightclubs, people from all over the metropolitan area continue to stop in for dinner.

Vincenzo Bellini Club

WARD IN A SONG
ART & RED SKIES
NA BOTH IN TECH

COLUMBIA

WING

NOW SHOWING

The Great Bank Robbery

Credit: Ed Berra, Southwest Bank, now BMO Harris Bank

On Friday, April 24, 1953, at 10:19 a.m., 60-year-old Fred Bowerman waved a sawed-off shotgun, jumped on the cashier counter at Southwest Bank, and yelled, "This is a holdup! Everybody stand still!" Teller Alice Ruzicka complied, after she tapped the foot alarm. Three other tellers and a telephone repairman also notified police, whose closest car arrived on the scene two minutes later. Officers Melburn Stein and Robert Heitz confronted Bowerman and his two accomplices, who had managed to stuff $140,769 into a bag. The getaway driver had already driven away. After a 40-round exchange and tear gas, one of the accomplices shot himself rather than go to jail. Officer Heitz was shot by Bowerman, and Bowerman was downed by a bullet from Officer Stein after Bowerman took a hostage, who was spared a bullet but broke both her wrists when Bowerman shoved her to the ground. The remaining accomplice was arrested and wept in court upon receiving a 25-year sentence. Bowerman died a week after the robbery. Officer Heinz recovered nicely, and Officer Stein lived to be 97 years old.

Thanks in part to the sensational photographs taken by *St. Louis Post-Dispatch* reporter Jack January, who raced his car through the city to get to the scene, the visual foundation screamed potential to Hollywood producers. They filmed part of *The Great St. Louis Bank Robbery* movie on location at the bank, using some locals as, well, themselves. The 1959 film loosely retells the story of the robbery. Young Steve McQueen plays the would-be getaway driver, a Marquette University quarterback who took too many wrong turns in his young life, and Officer Stein makes a cameo appearance as himself, as do others from the St. Louis police force. It is a light, entertaining piece, especially for bank-heist movie enthusiasts.

Southwest Bank caught Bowerman's attention because it was a genuine community bank patronized by people and business owners from The Hill. The bank held millions in deposits and hundreds of thousands in cash. Ironically, police board president Mr. I. A. Long was present at the incident and later bought and operated Southwest Bank from 1953 to 1984. The bank's assets grew from $20 million to $110 million during that time. He became so influential as an astute banker that he affected interest rates for the entire country. He built a community bank through neighborhood investment and personal integrity that was deeply missed after he fully retired.

REAL AS THE SCREAMING HEADLINES!
TRUE AS THE BULLETS THAT WROTE THEM!

Story Behind the
Great Southwest Bank Raid!

THE GREAT
ST. LOUIS
BANK ROBBERY

PLANNED
LIKE
CLOCKWORK...
GOES OFF
LIKE A
TIME BOMB!

STEVE McQUEEN · CRETE · DEHTH · MOLLY McCARTHY and the St. Louis Police Department

Credit: Cory Weaver

Credit: Cory Weaver

Credit: Cory Weaver

Credit: Jill Halpin

THE HILL TODAY

The Hill enclave remained resilient through several economic and societal challenges over its 130-year history. It survived the mines, attempts to dismantle its health through sludge dumps, a drive-in theater, highway intrusion, and absentee landlords. Even as the neighborhood has confidently moved into the 21st century, there seems to be a sense of loss. That network of kin and adoptive kin relations that made The Hill that fun little Italian neighborhood is weakening from the strain of extension. However, perhaps as with every previous prognostication, the farewells are premature.

PIAZZA IMO

Piazza Imo sits directly across the street from St. Ambrose Parish on Marconi Avenue. It is a piazza invoking the ubiquitous plazas at the center of towns and villages across all of Italy. Complete with a grand fountain boasting triumphant horses and leaping fishes, the piazza welcomes all. The cascading fountain and dedicated benches provide an inviting space for friendly chats. Religious statues offer the pious a tranquil place for reflection.

Dedicated in 2019, Piazza Imo is the largest privately financed public space project in Hill history. Guided by Monsignor Bommarito, it is funded by major benefactors, Hill-based businesses, and The Hill community through small individual contributions dedicated to family and loved ones. The space will be appreciated by residents and visitors alike for generations to come.

Credit: Barbara Northcott

THE HILL AS A PLACE TO LIVE

How one sees The Hill as a place to live depends on how one looks at it.

Imagining a day on The Hill for a resident rather than a visitor lends insight. A typical resident's day on The Hill might start with 6:30 a.m. weekday mass at St. Ambrose. They could take a quick stroll through the piazza to complete their pious reflections and get ready for the day. They would then exercise with a run through the neighborhood or at the neighborhood Y. They could go to one of the bakeries to pick up a treat for their co-workers or bread for the evening meal. They may stop at one of the grocers for some olive oil, dried pasta, or premium canned tomatoes for tonight's sauce, and run into a grade-school friend doing the same. After a conversation with the contractor who is rehabbing their porch or bathroom, they let his workers in to start the project. Before leaving for the office, they drop off a promised auction item for the school's fundraiser. They finish work in time to attend a community or church group planning meeting for next month's event.

ST. AMBROSE
Open House
• by mary balmer •

They return home for a quick meal, then walk the dog before settling in for the evening. Somewhere during the day, they called their elderly neighbor to be sure she is all right. They made plans to play bocce the next night at Milo's or the Bocce Club or to go to one of the restaurants' happy hours. If they have children, multiply the activity by three to include school functions and responsibilities. On Saturdays, most residents yield to visitors in the stores and restaurants. Though Yogi Berra was referring to Ruggeri's Restaurant when he said "It's too crowded, nobody goes there anymore," it remains the general sentiment for not venturing beyond the backyard on a beautiful Saturday afternoon on The Hill. Besides, pals from half of the block will be gathering at a neighbor's for barbeque at 6 p.m.

Piazzo Imo

 Claude Breckwoldt designed the Piazza Imo front gates. He was a student of Rudolph Torrini, who designed *The Italian Immigrants* statue standing in front of St. Ambrose across the street from the piazza.

Credit: Barbara Northcott

NEIGHBORHOOD REFLECTIONS

As with any long-standing community, the stories we tell sustain us across generations. It is a treat to hear first-person accounts of the past in the smallest details or the grandest episodes. Tales of the priest who carted students to ball games in the car they called the Green Hornet, the night almost half of the St. Louis Blues hockey team dropped in at the neighborhood tavern, the elderly neighbor who danced a mean jitterbug and macarena, or renaming a city street after local legends create a familiarity that binds. These are the stories that create a neighborhood by lending insight into who we are, where we've been, and where we're going.

WEST SIDE STORY

by Joe DeGregorio

At the end of World War II, GIs came home to St. Louis wanting to restart their lives and careers, get married, and have children. What many found in their old ethnic neighborhoods was a severe housing and apartment shortage, forcing many to move elsewhere, usually the suburbs. The Hill was an exception, with dozens of acres of vacant lands, especially to the west before Hampton and north before reaching the factories off Manchester. That land included the abandoned clay mines and of course "the Dump," allegedly the dumping grounds for the 1904 World's Fair. It was here that many of The Hill's Greatest Generation and others bought newly constructed homes, which in my opinion helped to preserve the almost total Italian ethnicity of the neighborhood for another generation while other Irish, Polish, Hungarian, etc., neighborhoods were in demographic decline. Along the western Shaw, Daggett, Sublette, Dugan, and Bischoff corridors, frame house after frame house, with some brick ones thrown into the mix, started rising in the 1950s. Sections named Stephen's Court and Berra Court sprung up. It is here where the story of several boyhood friends and neighbors on the 5600 block of Bischoff begins.

Chris Lamperti, Jerry Bazzetta, Anthony Zona, Joey DeGregorio, Tony Caputa (deceased), and occasionally David Villani spent many a happy summer day "on the block," with frequent jaunts to Macklind Field, then officially known as Vigo Park. And, yes, we messed with John DuPa's house like everyone else. We never thought of ourselves as special or elite just because we lived in brand-new homes.

And that Lombard versus Sicilian thing? I can't recall that ever being a factor in our friendship, although we do remember older folks sometimes talking about it. Recently, I was able to gather Chris and Jerry at my home in South County for recollections of those days, amidst a terribly played game of Wiffle ball and then a great dinner at Ronnie Grimoldi's place, Dulany's. Unfortunately, Anthony, who recently moved back from Seattle to the area, couldn't make it due to work commitments. But I'm certain he shares our collective memories.

We did some corkball, soccer in the alleys, flips, swings, backyard pools, and hide-and-seek of course. But our major forms of entertainment were Wiffle ball, horseshoes, and Monopoly in someone's basement (often Anita Regalia's) when it was too hot to play outside. Chris remembers us making dams. Dams? That's right! The rest of us almost forgot. Nobody initially had garages so they all washed their cars on the street, creating a steady flow of water. We pushed the loose gravel to the curb and made huge (for us) dams to block the water. We didn't realize our homes were built on the area's largest clay mine, until one day a large sinkhole filled with water appeared at the end of the block. We usually had no restrictions from Mom about going out to play as long as we got home in time for supper. Jerry remembered going to the Dump and searching for fool's gold. We all remembered broken cups, plates, and medicine bottles sometimes oozing out of the ground. Some memories that coincided with those of the Eastsiders included bike rides to Hampton Village ("car coming!") or to Forest Park for crawfishing, telephone party lines ("Joey, get off the phone or I'll tell your mother!"), visits to nana and papa just a few blocks east of us (or in Chris's case, a couple of houses east), pickup football on the nearest empty lot, and watching the older folks play bocce. Every adult was addressed as "Mr." or "Mrs." Other collective memories included the nearest store, Bandera's, at Bischoff and Sublette (it looked like something out of the early 1900s); going to Fassi's

to get bread, eggs, or milk and having them "put it on the books"; green vegetable truck; and "Tony the Milkman" (we later found out his real name wasn't Tony). We remembered the Lamperti's having the first known TV on the block and going over at 4 p.m. to watch *The Three Stooges* and *Flash Gordon*. Mary and Charlie Bazzetta had the third house built on the block, and she remembered the commotion of all the construction. But eventually as families moved in and kids were raised, there was nothing but children running in and out of houses all day. One thing we were not allowed to do was play near the houses being built. We had fewer gardens than the Eastsiders, since most were too busy starting careers and raising families. You would think that the greatest common ground for us and other Hill kids was Macklind Field, but we thought it was really the Columbia show's Wednesday afternoon matinees. We all remembered going to Mrs. Zona's nice brick house to play on some afternoons, and we remembered her great homemade snacks.

Finally, just in case some of you Eastsiders (George Venegoni) were jealous of our new digs, remember that we had to walk the farthest to school, to church, to the gym, to the Columbia show, to the Palace Bowl, and in all kinds of weather. OK, OK, we'll concede that we had the shortest walk/bike ride to Clifton Park, with it's nice stocked pond and great sledding.

of-the-oven freshness

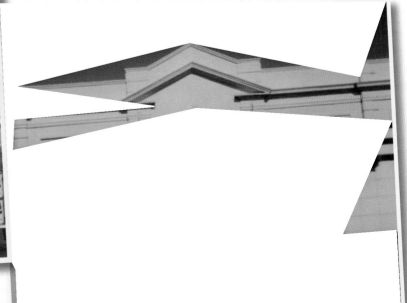

THE NEIGHBORHOOD DIALECT

by Joe DeGregorio and Paul DeGregorio

The Italian language used today was standardized across Italy in the mid-1800s, so the regional dialect was the first language of many Italian immigrants to the US. Formal Italian was a second language if it was used at all. As a result, the dialect was spoken in most early immigrant homes. Pigeons and hatchets . . . Anyone native to The Hill over 50 years old knows the context of these two words. They refer to the Lombard dialect and the Sicilian dialect spoken on The Hill by the early immigrants.

The Lombard and Sicilian dialects share little in common in terms of vocabulary, pronunciation, or even cadence. To the unfamiliar ear, the Lombard dialect emulated the cooing of a pigeon, while the Sicilian dialect tended to abruptly finish words sounding like chopping, thus hatchet. Since we were encouraged to speak English only, we quickly lost our ear for the old language, which was mostly gone, leaving the baby boomer generation with many words and phrases that were known and uttered phonetically. When Hill natives visiting the regions of their ancestors attempted the dialect, they brought on giggles and smiles of a time long gone.

We even make ourselves giggle a little when we use these old terms:

meeska—a term of exasperation, or when stretched to *meeeesska*, expresses amazement

mensa, mensa—doing so-so

see-thu-dee—be quiet or stop, can start the phrase with "Ai"

Madre Mia—momma, also more common "momma mia"

Ah Madon—Oh Madonna, another term of exasperation

bone jerno—good morning

oan-yun—onion

ban-yaa—the sauce, or gravy, to dip your bread

vatheenay—what we heard when an annoyed relative told us to scoot, often with a wink

bambeanno—baby, often used incorrectly for girls too

sangwich—what grandma wanted to make you when visiting, can also use "sam-ich"

stupeedoe—dumb or lame

bahs-lee-go—basil, a must in everyone's garden

perfetto—perfect

my-ya—white tank-top undershirt

bad-aa-tuh—hat

shee-vatz—slippers

zink—sink

fa bene—all is good

farmiola—someone with no manners

bobu stupido—someone who's done a very dumb thing

testa duda—hardhead, stubborn

baccausu—home bathroom

rumpa baldi—someone causing trouble (in context, either teasing or serious)

Buongiorno

MONSIGNOR POLIZZI

by Rio Vitale

I was baptized by Father Salvatore Polizzi (now Monsignor Polizzi) on The Hill at St. Ambrose Church in 1958. To my family, he was more than a parish priest; he is my mother's first cousin, and they both grew up in Little Italy, the downtown St. Louis Italian neighborhood. By the mid- to late 1960s, there was little remaining of Little Italy or the Italian church downtown. Father Polizzi was not going to let that happen to The Hill, and he did everything he could to improve and preserve our neighborhood. My family would often visit Father Polizzi's mother, Rosalia, and she would tell us what was going on behind the scenes at the rectory. During the 1970s, Father Polizzi had longer hair and a rather large mustache. He gained notoriety in the 1960s and 1970s, as an activist, first by stopping a drive-in theater from being built on The Hill. Then

he limited the number of billboards around the neighborhood. He prevented a company called Nation Lead from dumping effluent from lead mines into the abandoned coal mines under The Hill. His crowning achievement was fighting the federal government and moving the construction of Interstate 44. The archbishop grew concerned about his physical appearance and told him to shave his mustache if he wanted to continue teaching at the seminary. Father Polizzi is an obedient servant to God and the community, but he was not happy with this request. He shaved his mustache and put the whiskers in an envelope with a letter to the archbishop, telling him that they should be kept in his personnel file. If not for Monsignor Polizzi, The Hill would not have survived as it is today.

A BABY BOOMER'S RETROSPECTIVE

By George Venegoni

As members of the nation's post–World War II baby boomer generation who grew up on The Hill, nearly all of my friends and I are products of our second-generation Italian American parents. We reflect their values, as well as the values of our aunts, our uncles, and the friends of our second-generation relatives with whom we were in regular contact. That generation has been labeled by journalist and author Tom Brokaw as America's "greatest generation" for their perseverance during the Great Depression and for their courage and patriotism during World War II. I am proud to know that their core values, all heavily seasoned with an ethnic Italian flavor, have shaped who I am today. I believe that to be the case with my fellow baby boomers from The Hill.

I was the oldest of four children born to Angelo and Angela (Finocchiaro) Venegoni. My sister, Antoinette, my brothers Gerard and Angelo, and I were born out of what was often jokingly referred to on The Hill as a "mixed marriage." But in the early 20th century, it was not a joking matter. My mom's parents were from the Sicilian towns of Acireale and Giarre, and my dad's parents were from the town of Cuggiono, in the Lombard region of Northern Italy. Going back to the early days of the Italians in St. Louis, these two groups did not mix

well. By the time I made my entry into this world, however, the previous mistrust and occasional animosity between early Sicilian and Lombard immigrants had subsided considerably. If not for that fact, I would not be here today.

My fond childhood memories are less often dominated by a sense of my "Italian–ness"—if there is such a word—than they are by Catholic and 1950s America worldviews. I

grew up during an era that I now consider to be the golden age of America, of St. Louis, and of The Hill. It was a postwar period of economic optimism and unshakeable American patriotism.

My biggest takeaway from this is that I was fortunate to have made many lifelong friendships during that golden age in that close-knit neighborhood known as The Hill. These early friendships have withstood the test of time. They have remained gratifying to my friends and me throughout our adult lives, all resulting from our shared Italian "American–ness" in a close-knit neighborhood. Several guys from my grade school class and I meet regularly for breakfast at Rigazzi's, the longest-operating restaurant on The Hill.

After my parents, my secondary heroes as a kid back then were introduced to me via the television screen. They were courageous men of action, good guys such as the Lone Ranger ("the daring and resourceful masked rider of the plains"), the Cisco Kid ("Here's adventure! Here's romance! Here's O. Henry's Robin Hood of the Old West!"), Wild Bill Hickok ("Kellogg's, the greatest name in cereal, presents Wild Bill Hickok!"), and Superman ("strange visitor from another planet who came to Earth with powers and abilities far beyond

Nani, Aunyya, and me

those of mortal men, and who fights a never-ending battle for truth, justice, and the American way").

Above all else, St. Ambrose Parish was the glue that held The Hill together. It remains so today. The parish church and school have always played a major role in preserving the ethnic Italian traditions of the neighborhood. For hundreds of kids who grew up just like I did, St. Ambrose was the focal point of our young lives. It was instrumental in contributing to my outlook on life and in shaping the person I would one day become. In those days, St. Ambrose Church and The Hill were nearly synonymous.

Nanu and me

A SIMPLE LIFE FULL OF ADVENTURE

by George Venegoni

Besides playing Cowboys, or Army, or various forms of baseball, another of my favorite childhood activities was to go exploring in "the Dump" with my friends. What might be termed the "Upper" Dump was very close to my house. It was an area that ran behind the factories along the 5200 and 5300 blocks of Northrup, stretched north behind the factories for several yards, and then sloped gradually downward for about 100 yards or more toward the River des Peres. It was a weeded and rocky wasteland, but it was paradise for adventurous and, for the most part, unsupervised kids. In those days, there was also a "Lower" Dump located north of Shaw Avenue and west of Macklind Avenue (prior to Highway 44 construction). The Lower Dump was where most of my friends who lived in the newer homes in the western section of The Hill did their exploring. Sometimes we went investigating simply out of boredom. At other times, groups of us would "play jungle," toy rifles in hand, imagining that we were characters in the popular 1950s TV show for kids, *Ramar of the Jungle*. There were several clusters of tall weeds growing behind those factories. Many of the wild dandelions were taller than I was! At least it seemed that way.

Some of my friends who frequented the Lower Dump would build forts with bricks and tree branches, and they would have rock fights or snowball fights during wintertime. My next-door neighbor "Butchie" Puricelli and his friends would sneak potatoes from home, encase them in mud, and drop them into small campfires that they had built. They would then enjoy "baked" potatoes for their lunches.

George riding a rocking horse in his backyard with cap and pistol

Credit: George Venegoni

As you might well imagine, our parents—especially our moms—regularly warned us not to play in the Dump. This was partly due to the Dump's relative vastness in size, the thick, insect-infested weeds that dominated the landscape, and the indeterminate types of hazardous materials that were dumped back there by workers from the factories on Northrup. There were also varieties of slithering and creeping reptiles occupying the turf, just waiting to strike a kid who disturbed their habitat. There were hornets and grasshoppers in the Dump, and those 1950s grasshoppers were gigantic! They were large enough to carry a small kid away! I believe that, I really do!

For most of the guys in my neighborhood, however, Macklind Field (officially designated by the city as Vigo Park, and later renamed Berra Park) was absolutely the place to be, especially in the summertime. During summer afternoons in those uncomplicated, innocent days of our youth in the 1950s and 1960s, you might find 150 to 200 guys and gals at the park, involved in a host of city-sponsored activities, playing baseball or soccer, or just hanging out. The same can be said for weekday evenings when the park hosted men's slow-pitch softball games. Teenagers and preteens were everywhere.

In those days, there wasn't a Walgreen's or CVS at seemingly every major intersection in St. Louis, like there is today. But within walking distance, we had Serra's Drugstore (where I bought all of my Superman comic books), owned by Mr. Lou

Cousin Lou Ferrario with Budweiser Clydesdales in front of his tavern on Pattison
Credit: George Venegoni

Serra, and Cunetto's Pharmacy, owned by Vince and Joe Cunetto. We didn't need urgent-care centers because both Dr. Montani, who lived in the neighborhood, and Dr. LoPiccolo had offices at Daggett and Marconi.

And those saloons! There may have been more Italian American–owned corner taverns and saloons on The Hill during the 1950s than there were grocery stores. One of them was Ferrario's, owned by my older cousin, Lou Ferrario, located on Pattison Avenue.

As a kid, I could often be found, usually on Saturday afternoons, seated at the bar at Ferrario's Tavern—with my dad, of course. I would be sipping from a cold bottle of Hires root beer, while my dad would be sipping from a "short beer" glass of Busch Bavarian and chatting with one or more of his Ferrario nephews or other neighborhood men who were also seated at the bar. I might also be found on my own at my cousin Lou's saloon during the summertime, laying down a dime on the bar for a cold Pepsi-Cola and another dime for a Lakeshire hot dog, which I would consume outside, sitting on the curb. With all the *delizioso*, lovingly prepared Italian food available at home or in neighborhood restaurants, goofy little Georgie Venegoni preferred a saloon hot dog! I did say that I was American, right?

Although I was the product of Italian Americans in a mixed marriage, I did not have the benefit of hearing and learning the unique and colorful Lombard phrases uttered on The Hill. My mom was of Sicilian lineage, so my dad did not use the Lombard dialect, or "Hill-speak," when talking to her around the house. Nor did I pick up any Sicilian phrases from my mom, for the same reason. In our household, all of the members of my immediate family communicated with each other exclusively in English. When my dad and my uncles would carry on animated conversations on various subjects, the conversations would typically shift back and forth between English, Italian, and Hill-speak. Italian was always spoken when my grandma entered into the conversation. I could never understand anything that any of them were saying.

On these visits, Nana Regina Venegoni would always offer me candy from an assortment she kept in a bowl in her kitchen, and one of my uncles would pour me a glass of "white sodee" from a green thirty-ounce Blue Ridge soda bottle. Blue Ridge Soda was the soda company that was owned by the Oldani brothers and was located on the eastern edge of the neighborhood, at Shaw and Kingshighway. And about that vino rosso: my dad and my uncles sipped it the

manly, old-fashioned way—from small glasses, not from pretentious, long-stemmed, bubble-shaped wine glasses. *Meeska*! No way! Nor could they have cared less if their wine breathed prior to taking that first sip. Back in those simpler times, I don't believe that wine had yet evolved into an entity with human attributes, including the ability to breathe. But I could be wrong about that.

Visiting my Sicilian grandparents, Agata "Tina" and Alfio Finocchiaro, who my siblings and I called "Nani" (pronounced Nonni) and "Nanu" (Nonnu), was an altogether different experience from visiting the home of Nana Regina Venegoni. In her younger days, Nani worked as a seamstress at a dress factory in downtown St. Louis, so she had learned to speak English very well but with a slight accent. In our very young years, Nani made much of the clothing for my siblings and me. Nanu's command of English was less polished, but he did communicate fairly well with us when he wanted to. He was a quiet man.

When we sat down to dinner with Nani, Nanu, Aunt Anna, and Uncle Salvatore, the kitchen table was not large enough to accommodate the four adults plus my sister and me, so the grandchildren's table consisted of an ironing board, covered with a folded bed sheet. After dinner, we were driven home by my Uncle Sal, or we would be picked up by my dad.

In my very early days at St. Ambrose, Nanu would often wait for me on Wilson after school and then walk me home. My mom, who did not drive, was home with my three younger siblings.

Nani's and Nanu's cucina is where I began to learn to cook . . . well, sort of. My cucina responsibilities at their house were prep work. They consisted of snapping fresh string beans in half (they never ate anything out of a can), breaking bundles

Grandma Venegoni's kitchen. *Front, left to right*: Gerard, Nana Regina, and Angelo. *Back, left to right*: Uncles Caesar, Lawrence, and George.

George's backyard. *Left to right*: Gerard, Antoinette, and George

of R & F capellini in half, and placing the strands of uncooked pasta in a bowl prior to them being placed into a pot of boiling salt water. Nani would never let me put the pasta in the pot of boiling water for fear that her little *picciriddu* might scald his precious little fingers.

The relationship between grandparents, parents, and children was a very special one in our close-knit, ethnic Italian neighborhood. The people of The Hill viewed raising children and grandchildren as an effort to be shared by the whole family. Often there were three generations of family members living under one roof. All these years later, when we reflect upon our upbringing, we cherish this feeling of family and sharing.

The Infamous Dump

Anyone born on The Hill after 1950 missed the dump experience. It was not a typical trash dump as the phrase is understood today. Rather, the dumps on The Hill encompassed large open tracts of fields where weeds, trees, plants, birds, and bugs flourished. One portion served as a cow pasture. Families used segments of the wild land to dispose of the ash from their coal-burning stoves and furnaces, while factories piled slag, or foundry waste, into mounds. Children from the same block, usually in groups of five to ten, would spend hours in the fields. They played games, climbed the mounds, explored, built clubhouses, and simply enjoyed being children.

FAMILY MEALS

by Joyce Clyne

I remember making ravioli in our basement. My grandfather had been a cook while serving in the US Army during World War I, so we had all of the kitchen utensils needed to make ravioli: a meat grinder (attached to a table), a rolling pin with one-by-two-inch squares, and a ravioli cutter wheel. I still have that ravioli cutter. My grandfather was also an avid hunter and fisherman, so he often prepared the ever-popular Lombard—and Hill neighborhood—dishes of polenta *coniglio* (rabbit stew) and polenta *rustida* (stewed pork).

Grandpa also harvested fresh vegetables from his garden, which covered one whole side of our long backyard. He grew tomatoes, swiss chard, potatoes, carrots, radishes, parsley, basil, and other herbs. He also picked mushrooms in Forest Park, dried them in the sun, and then stored them in jars in the cellar beneath our front porch. We also had grape arbors (*topia*), and I remember that in summertime I used to help out with making grape jelly.

My grandparents and later my mom often prepared *minestra* (Lombard dialect for minestrone) soup. My grandparents always had a bowl of soup and a small glass of wine to start off each meal. Another of our traditions was to have ravioli, along with Oldani salami, swiss cheese, and buns (*migets*) from Amighetti's Bakery on Christmas, New Year's, and Easter. I have continued that family tradition today with my own family of fifteen.

THE SPIRIT OF ST. JOSEPH

by Tony Zona

The St. Ambrose Church calendar, posted prominently in our kitchen, was in large part a reminder of our Italian traditions: St. Joseph altars, with special foods like Sicilian multibean pasta (fava beans and chickpeas) and the special breads that were baked and then blessed by the priests; Easter Week devotions, which were so invested with ritual and spiritual meaning; Rogation Day parades in springtime to bless backyard gardens, reminiscent of prayers offered in Italy for

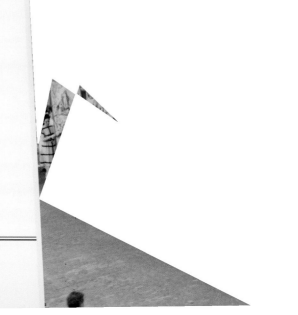

bountiful harvests; Corpus Christi processions in June; and the Advent season and Christmastime.

Just like in Italy, so many of our neighbors and friends had gardens in their yards, a custom which was very common not only in Italy, but also in most of Western Europe. The Hill was also dotted with grape arbors, which supplied both fruit to eat and a welcome shaded area for outdoor family meals during the summer months.

The Sicilian side of my family stomped grapes every summer (at least when I was young) and made a red table wine that could be enjoyed by all. Even the young kids in the family always got a couple of fingers of red wine, mixed with water, with dinner on Sundays and on special occasions. Speaking of special occasions, I remember that every Christmas we had a delicacy that my family called *polipu*—octopus!

The Sicilian side of our family was patriarchal. For example, the men and kids were served first at large dinners. The women ate afterward. Kids were not supposed to utter a word during meals, and Grandpa LaFerla would give a stern look to anyone in violation of dinner etiquette.

THE CARDUCCI SISTERS

by Kathy Bagby

One day, many years ago, my sister Jan, my cousin Diana Bono, and I realized that if we did not learn to make cannoli and certain special family cookies, the art would be lost. So, during October of that year, we asked my mom and our aunts, the Carducci sisters, to teach us to make cannoli. My Aunts Josie Scarna, Lena Scarato, and Mary Baudo, along with my mom, Angela Antinoro, each brought my grandma's recipes with them. The Sicilian sisters were now on a mission.

My aunts' recipes differed slightly, some using butter, some margarine, and some Crisco, which affected the frying method, the time, and also the flavor. There were so many steps! Prepare the dough, roll it out, and then put it through the pasta machine to achieve the proper thickness. Then use an espresso coffee saucer to cut a round disc of dough to be folded around a wooden rod, secured with egg whites. Now the cannoli were ready to fry. We would only fry four at a time in a deep fryer.

When the shells were fried, the rods were removed, and the shells were placed on paper towels that were placed atop paper bags to help absorb the oil while cooling. Then we made the filling, which was a two-day process: day one to make the *mangiare bianco* and day two to add the ricotta. Everyone agreed that my mom's filling was the best.

After that first get-together to teach us—the next generation— we continued to meet every year, and my aunts would add a new cookie recipe or two each time. We would usually prepare seven or eight batches of twenty-five cannoli at these family gatherings. Everyone had enough for the upcoming holidays. The cannoli froze beautifully.

Growing up with Italian traditions and listening to the stories of each generation from The Hill is what makes us who we are. It's all about family, food, and faith.

CAN YOU TELL ME HOW TO GET TO THE HILL?
St. Louis's Most Visited Neighborhood

by Dea Hoover

When I moved to the neighborhood and was introducing myself at the neighborhood eateries, I had an unforgettable conversation with Adriana Fazio. She runs an amazing sandwich shop called Adriana's with her daughters Dianna, Suzie, and Tia across from Guido's Restaurant on Shaw. Adriana's is the only place I have found for homemade caponata, a beloved and labor-intensive Sicilian dish. I handed her my tour company business card, and she asked exactly where I was on Columbia. I explained that I lived across the street from Mr. Oldani and that technically I was on the Southwest Garden side of the street. Her response warmed my heart, "Oh don't worry about that. The Hill is expansive. You're part of the neighborhood." Being from a small Missouri town of a little under 3,000, I almost cried. I knew I had moved to a place not unlike my first home.

I also learned that I was not alone. Many transplants that have become involved in the neighborhood and join the community to keep The Hill traditions that attracted them to move here alive and well.

Jim Barnthouse, a descendant of Sicilian immigrants who arrived in New Orleans in the 1860s, recalls when he and his wife, Stephanie Scott, moved to the neighborhood. They walked out on their front porch to discover cookies from a neighbor welcoming them to The Hill. The gesture cemented the fact that after living in three other St. Louis city neighborhoods they had landed in the one that was going to be home. They too devote time and energy to neighborhood events and projects.

From my perspective as a tour operator, concierges, bell staff, front desk clerks, and visitor center volunteers hear this question every day: "Can you tell me how to get to The Hill?" The Hill's cuisine and shopping make it a must-visit place for many tourists. Explore St. Louis, the region's convention and visitor bureau, states that one of the most requested neighborhoods for visitor information is The Hill. Recently installed wayfinding signs along the highways and thoroughfares of St. Louis now direct the uninitiated to the neighborhood. Until then, it had been the best unkept secret in town!

Lidia Bastianich, author of *Lidia's Italy in America*, stops frequently to visit the shops and bask in the old-style feel of the neighborhood. Restaurants on The Hill know that over 80 percent of their clientele come from outside the neighborhood to experience one of the last authentic Italian neighborhoods in the United States. The demand is so great that three local tour companies give tours of the neighborhood, and numerous national and international groups find their way to the neighborhood for lunch or dinner or to shop at many of the independent, family-run businesses. In the early 1900s, The Hill developed as what we now refer to in urban planning as a mixed-use neighborhood. And so it remains.

The narrow streets and hilly landscape make for a nice stroll. Berra Park is the gathering location for most events. With beautiful new restrooms, a playground, and spacious grounds located on one of the widest streets, Macklind Avenue, the park invites you to have a great time.

Anyone looking for a renovation project can find the opportunity to revive a home if they work diligently to find an owner willing to part with their property. Jim Barnthouse and wife, Stephanie Scott, had their 1891 home featured in the 2019 *St. Louis Magazine*'s Top 10 Most Beautiful Homes. Built by US Builder, a company that built homes for miners, its first occupants were a German baker and then an Irish painter. Around 1894, the boarding house was filled with Italians. The first Italian family moved into the home around 1904 and continued renting to boarders. They owned dump trucks, and thus there was a large garage. Apparently, they also built the garages for their neighbors.

The familiar sound of St. Ambrose Catholic Church's bells announcing mass, as well as the time of day, gives the feeling of living in a small town, although The Hill is located in the heart of a metro area of 2.8 million. St. Ambrose Church also marks the epicenter of this Catholic Italian neighborhood, and the latest addition across the street, Piazza Imo, completes the European atmosphere of this small area nestled in the heart of a 66-square-mile city. Taking off in any direction from the epicenter of Daggett and Marconi places the visitor near bakeries, Italian grocers, a soap maker, a beauty salon, law offices, a private bocce club, and the public bocce courts at Milo's, the neighborhood gathering place owned by our city alderman.

Not only is it a tourist destination, but it's also a residential neighborhood attractive to those with a love for home renovation and people who enjoy a small-town atmosphere with the amenities of living in a city. Today, this multifaceted neighborhood attracts a wide variety of new residents with its tight streets that calm traffic, yards that allow for neighborly interaction, and a strong central business district.

All generations find benefits to residing in an area full of social, sporting, religious, and shopping opportunities. Public bocce courts at several establishments and the private Italia-America Bocce Club allow for all generations to mix and mingle while participating in a lifelong sport. Many people find themselves moving back to the neighborhood and appreciating the tight-knit community where they were raised, or perhaps they were drawn back by fond memories of visiting their grandparents.

Some Italians from other cities find themselves landing in this spot due to the familiarity and link to their heritage. Interestingly, people from Sicily and the Lombard region are still moving into the area. Seeing the *Il Pensiero* Italian-language newspaper, seeing street banners and fire hydrants painted like the Italian flag, and hearing bocce pronounced properly extends an unspoken invitation to make their new home in a place not so unlike their old one.

Small markets, bakeries, coffee and gelato shops, and retail shopping all within a mile of each other allow for a car-free lifestyle and the time to stroll down the street and meet up with neighbors. Golf carts play a major role in transporting neighbors to their favorite gathering spots, where they can always find a place to park on the sidewalk!

Credit: Jill Halpin

JOHN VIVIANO & SONS
IMPORTERS OF ITALIAN FOODS WHOLESALE AND RETAIL

"On The Hill" in St. Louis

Tomato·Basil Pasta Sauce

Credit: Jill Halpin

NET WT 2 oz (1LB 1 OZ) 936g

RECIPES

Families have their own specialty dishes and preparation style, often reflecting their ancestral region or village. While written recipes guide the cook, there is equal focus on how the dish looks, feels, smells, and tastes in order to prepare it correctly. Cooking in an Italian American household is a shared endeavor. Dad proudly prepares his grandma's pasta sauce for Sunday dinner. Men and women visit The Hill's grocers to purchase ingredients for evening supper, engaging in conversations about a new brand of olive oil or the different saffron packets imported from Italy. Italian cuisine is satisfying because cooks observe simple rules: use fresh ingredients and if it tastes good, don't change it. Enjoy the following recipes; play with them, perfect them, make them your own. *Mangia!*

RECIPES

PASTA ALLA GRICIA

1 lb. spaghetti or other long, thin pasta
2 tbl. extra virgin olive oil
1/4 lb. thinly sliced guanciale, sliced into 1/2-inch strips
1 cup finely grated Pecorino Romano, plus more for serving
1 tbl. coarsely ground black pepper, or more as desired

Bring a large pot of salted water to a boil and cook the pasta about a minute short of package directions.

Meanwhile, put the olive oil and guanciale in a large skillet. Set the skillet over medium heat and cook until the lard has rendered and the guanciale is softened. Splash in a little water from the pasta cooking pot to keep the guanciale cooking slowly. Do not let it brown. You want the meat to be soft and translucent and the fat and starchy water to form a sauce. Swirl in splashes of water as needed to keep the guanciale moist.

When the pasta is cooked al dente, use tongs to lift it out of the water, leaving some water clinging to it, and drop into the skillet. Increase the heat to high. Vigorously toss and stir the pasta with the pork fat, slowly adding more pasta water as you go, until the pasta is coated in a silky sauce. You may need to use as much as a cup of water, added a little at a time, so it incorporates into the sauce.

Remove the skillet from the heat and sprinkle the cheese in one layer over the hot pasta. Pause for a moment to let it begin to melt (it will begin to deflate from the steam beneath), then toss everything together until the cheese becomes part of the sauce. Grind black pepper over the pasta—be generous with the pepper. Serve with more grated cheese.

Volpi Foods

ITALIAN CASSATA

(Custard Cake)

1/2 gal. milk (reserve 1 1/2 cup milk cold)
1 jar maraschino cherries (drain, rinse)
1 lb. ricotta cheese
1 1/2 cup cornstarch
1 1/2 cup sugar
3 drops cinnamon oil
2 tsp. vanilla extract
12 oz. slivered almonds (toasted)
2 large Hershey chocolate bars with almonds
2 pound cakes (slice 1/2-inch thick)

Simmer milk (do not boil), add extracts and sugar. Stir until dissolved. Dissolve cornstarch with reserve milk. Add to liquid, stir until thick. Remove from heat. Beat ricotta in a bowl until smooth, add to the warm pudding, blend well.

Place cut pound cake in 9" × 13" oblong dish. Layer cake, pour pudding, spread evenly, sprinkle shaved chocolate and almonds. Alternate with second layer, same as the first. Decorate with chocolate, almonds, and cherries (cut in half).

Note: Darrell recommends using either liquid cinnamon, which can be bought at DiGregorio's, or cinnamon stix when heating the milk. He increases the ricotta in larger versions to two pounds.

Darrell Fuse

SICILIAN STYLE FRIED CARDUNI

2 stalks of Carduni, about 2–3 pounds

4 eggs

For breading mixture:

¼ cup flour

1½ cups of Progresso Italian bread crumbs (or DiGregorio's bread crumbs)

8 oz. box of Progresso Italian panko flakes (about 2 cups)

1 tsp. salt

½ tsp. pepper

1 tsp. parsley flakes

1 tsp. garlic powder or granulated garlic

¼ cup grated Parmesan cheese (or mix of Parm/Romano)

For frying:

¾ canola oil and ¼ olive oil ratio (optional sesame oil vs. olive oil)

Two lemons

Cut one to two inches off the bottom of the stalk and about ½ inch from the top. It's very important to trim the edges of stalks containing thorns, using a sharp knife slicing the outer threads. Rinse the stalks thoroughly.

Cut the stalks into about three-inch chunks. You may split the wider lower portions in half.

Using a large pot with salted water, medium boil the cut Carduni for 35 minutes (if you like them a bit crunchy, boil for 25 minutes). Drain and let cool (if you taste them now, they will taste exactly like an artichoke heart).

Whisk eggs in one bowl and mix breading mixture well in another bowl.

Dip the cooled pieces in the eggs for a generous coat and then firmly in the bread mixture, coating both sides. Then place them on a tray prior to frying. Heat a large deep frying pan with ¾ canola oil to ¼ olive oil ratio for total of 1 inch of oil (about 360 degrees).

Deep fry the Carduni for at least 2–3 minutes or until golden brown, filling the pan as much as you can safely handle. Using a large slotted spoon, let as much oil drain from them as possible when removing and then place on cookie trays that have a layer of paper towels on bottom to soak up oil. As the pan fills up, put paper towels on each successive layer. After you think paper towels have done their job, remove them and squeeze on a generous portion of lemon juice. Serve with lemon wedges as either an appetizer or a vegetable dish complementing the main course. Five pieces will suffice for each newcomer to this delicious treat and many more for consuming veterans. Makes about 40 three-inch pieces. You can cut recipe in half for 20 pieces.

Joe DeGregorio

MELANZANE ALLA MOZZARELLA

12 slices of eggplant cut ¾ inch thick

12 tomato slices

12 fresh basil leaves

12 thin slices of mozzarella

¼ cup extra virgin olive oil

Fresh ground pepper

Sprinkle the eggplant slices with salt on each side. Place them between two plates, add a weight on top, and let the eggplant drain for approximately an hour. Lightly salt the tomato slices and set aside.

Pat each slice of eggplant dry, then cook on a hot grill until tender (a few minutes on each side). Arrange them on a serving dish. Top each with a tomato slice, mozzarella slice, and a basil leaf. Drizzle with oil, season with salt and pepper, and serve.

Sam Martorelli

ZAMPE DI MAIALE

(Grandma's pigs' feet in tomato sauce)

6 cups of meatless red sauce

3–4 pounds of pigs' feet (fresh or frozen)

Salt and pepper

Make about six cups of your favorite meatless red sauce.

Take 3–4 pounds of fresh or frozen pigs' feet (can be obtained or ordered at DiGregorio's market, Kenrick's meat market, and grocery stores catering to Mexican Americans). You can ask them to split the pigs' feet down the middle for easier handling.

After thoroughly rinsing in warm water, soak and slow boil the pigs' feet in salted water for 10–12 minutes, picking out any bristles that may remain.

Dry pork with paper towels, then salt and pepper. Place pork in pan with enough oil to brown on all sides. Remove and place in pot of sauce. Simmer for one hour or more until tender. Remove from pot with slotted spoon, and place in serving bowl. Skim any oil off top of sauce, and serve with your choice of pasta. You can also substitute ham hocks, pork roast, pork chops, or ribs if you wish to make it more palatable for your non-purist guests. Serves 4–6.

Joe DeGregorio

RISOTTO

(with saffron, shrimp, sausage, and chicken)

2 lbs. albino rice

7–8 saffron capsules

2 32 oz. cartons bone broth

1 lb. peeled, deveined shrimp

10–15 sliced mushrooms

1 lb. chicken breasts, cooked and diced

1 cup white wine

1 stick of butter

1 diced red pepper

1 lb. of Italian sausage

2 medium onions, sweet

Sea salt and pepper to taste

Sauté mushrooms and diced onions in some of the melted butter. Add rice and wine. Stir until blended.

Add saffron capsules. Add sea salt and pepper. Mix well.

Heat the chicken broth. Add to the rice and simmer until cooked (25–30 minutes).

Sauté the remaining ingredients in a little more wine and butter. Add to the rice.

Optional: sprinkle with grated Pecorino or Parmesan cheese.

Serves about 10 with some leftovers expected.

Tina Crouppen

TIRAMISU

3 egg yolks

3 tbl. superfine sugar

1⅓ cups Marsala or brandy

¼ cup very strong espresso coffee

8 oz. mascarpone cheese (room temperature)

½ cup cream

1 egg white

4 oz. savoiardi or ladyfingers

Make a zabaglione by beating egg yolks and sugar on top of a double boiler until ivory in color. Add ⅓ cup Marsala or brandy and whisk over simmering water until the mixture starts to thicken. Remove from heat and let it cool.

Stir together the espresso and mascarpone. Whip the cream until soft peaks form and set aside. In another bowl, beat the egg white until stiff and gently fold the egg white into the zabaglione.

Dip the ladyfingers into the remaining Marsala or brandy and arrange in a single layer in the bottom of a 9-in. bowl. Cover with half the mascarpone, then half the zabaglione, and half the cream. Repeat the layers, finishing with the cream. Refrigerate for several hours until thoroughly chilled. Serve.

Sam Martorelli

SICILIAN CHICKEN

For Sicilian Sauce (We call this a sauce, but it's really a dressing to be used sparingly to taste)

3⁄4 cup fresh lemon juice

1 cup extra virgin olive oil

1 tbl. fresh chopped garlic

2 tsp. dried oregano

1 tsp. coarse black pepper

1 tbl. kosher salt

(adjust all ingredients to taste)

Add lemon juice, fresh garlic, oregano, kosher salt, and pepper to mixing bowl. Slowly whisk in olive oil until well blended. Refrigerate any unused sauce.

For the Chicken

4–8 oz. boneless and skinless chicken breast (marinate chicken in Favazza's House Italian dressing overnight or at least a couple hours)

1⁄4 cup olive oil (to dip chicken before bread crumbs)

Seasoned Italian bread crumbs (to coat chicken before grilling)

Dip chicken lightly into olive oil and dredge in Italian bread crumbs before grilling.

After chicken is completely grilled on both sides, stir and spoon a couple of tablespoons Sicilian sauce over the top before serving, preferably while chicken is still hot so it absorbs the sauce. Enjoy!

Favazza's on The Hill

CIOPPINO MAJERUS

(Saint Louis University basketball coach Rick Majerus claimed that he has had this dish extensively all over the world and ours is the finest!)

2 tbl. chopped garlic

1⁄2 cup chopped red onion

1⁄4 cup (packed) chopped fresh basil

10 turns freshly ground black pepper

2 pinches crushed red pepper flakes

1 cup Chianti wine

1 can (28 oz.) San Marzano tomatoes hand crushed

1 cup strong lobster stock (or clam juice)

2 tbl. chopped fresh parsley

Salt to taste

Cook covered 15 minutes at a simmer.

Increase heat to medium and add:

1 cap saffron

8 large sea scallops

8 extra-large shrimp

8 oz. swordfish or other firm fish

16 fresh whole clams

16 large black mussels

1 cup cooked arborio rice

Extra clam juice as needed

Serve with toasted crusty Italian bread.

In large skillet, cook and stir garlic, onion, basil, black pepper, and red pepper until onion is transparent. Deglaze with wine. Heat and stir to loosen pieces of mixture from bottom of skillet. Add undrained tomatoes, stock, and spices.

Simmer, covered, 15 minutes. Add saffron, scallops, shrimp, swordfish, clams, mussels, and risotto. Cook over medium heat, covered, adding hot clam juice as needed. Clams and mussels have opened (all seafood should be cooked through). Serve in bowls, with Italian bread on the side for dipping. Serves 4 as main course or 8 as first course.

Chef LoRusso

POLENTA E SALSICCIA

Friuli Venezia Giulia is in the northeast region of Italy and borders Austria, Slovenia, and the Adriatic Sea. This recipe is connected with this region because of its Italian sausage—salsiccia. You can find salsiccia in any of the local delis on The Hill.

- 6 cups water
- Salt
- 2⅔ cups fine cornmeal
- 1½ lb. Italian sausages
- 3 tbl. butter
- 1 tbl. red wine vinegar

In a large saucepan, add 6 cups of water and a pinch of salt and bring to a boil. Sprinkle in the cornmeal, stirring constantly with a wooden spoon. Cook for 40 minutes while stirring frequently.

Prick the sausages with a fork. Melt butter in a skillet and add sausages. Fry for about 10 minutes, turning periodically. Once cooked, drizzle the red wine vinegar over sausages.

Spoon polenta onto a serving plate and top with sausages. Spoon melted sausage fat over the top. Serve right away. Enjoy!

Sam Martorelli

RAVIOLI END SOUP

- 2 46-ounce cans of chicken broth
- Chopped celery, carrots, and onion with the portions suitable to your particular needs and tastes
- 1 lb. of ravioli ends

Bring broth to a boil. Add chopped vegetables to broth. Lower heat to a simmer. Salt and pepper to taste. Cook until vegetables are almost tender. Add frozen ravioli ends, simmering until ravioli and vegetables are done, usually 8–10 minutes.

Nick and Patty Toscano

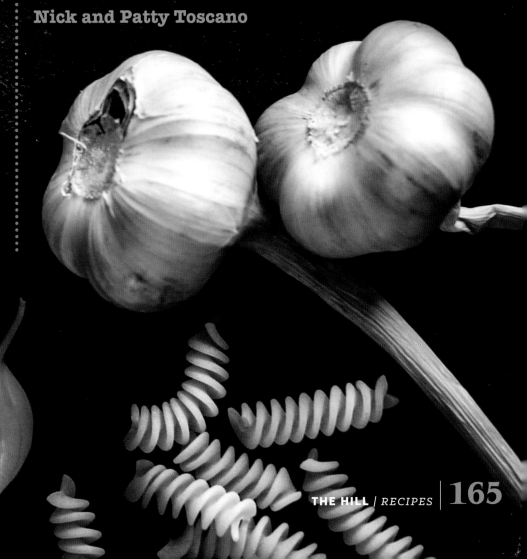

Credit: Barbara Northcott

SOURCES

Plotting the Land

Seppa, Nathan. "Metropolitan Life on the Mississippi," special to the *Washington Post*, March 12, 1997, p. H01.

"The Lewis and Clark Journey of Discovery," https://www.nps.gov/jeff/learn/historyculture/the-lewis-and-clark-journey-of-discovery.htm. Accessed February 18, 2020.

"The Gratiot League Square," http://faculty.webster.edu/corbetre/dogtown/history/gratiot.html.

Clay Mines

"May 17, 1849: The Great Fire That Changed the Face of St. Louis," https://www.stltoday.com/news/archives/may-the-great-fire-that-changed-the-face-of-st/article_ff8faca9-1ba5-5f52-9252-e8397b705240.html. Accessed February 29, 2020.

St. Ambrose Church

Fortieth Anniversary Historical Review: Brief Historical Sketches and Data of Saint Ambrose Parish, 1903–1943, p. 83.

"The Italian Immigrants," https://racstl.org/public-art/the-italian-immigrants/. Accessed March 8, 2020.

St. Ambrose School

Fortieth Anniversary Historical Review: Brief Historical Sketches and Data of Saint Ambrose Parish, 1903–1943.

Cheltenham Elementary School

Discovering African American St. Louis, edited by John A. Wright (St. Louis: Missouri Historical Society, 2002).

"Vashon School to be Sold By Board of Education," *St. Louis Post-Dispatch*, October 11, 1911, p. 4.

O'Fallon Technical High School

American Vocational Association, Pennsylvania State University, 1959, Volumes 34–35, p. 25. Digitized May 4, 2011.

Gateway STEM High School, https://www.slps.org/domain/11231 accessed August 27, 2020.

https://www.stltoday.com/news/local/govt-and-politics/clinton-initiative-volunteers-paint-plant-lay-carpet-at-st-louis-magnet-school/article_f30e448b-7eeb-5e6f-beab-bf277d65b2fb.html accessed 27 August 2020

Sacred Heart Villa

"Sacred Heart Villa Grotto," *Hill 2000*, January 1998.

"Sacred Heart Villa Provides Community Service," *Hill 2000*, December 1973.

Restaurants

JBF America's Classics. Accessed March 15, 2020.

McGuire, John. "Sala's Cafe Going the Way of 15-Cent Lunch," *St. Louis Post-Dispatch*, October 27, 1976, p. 1.

Local Businesses Sustain a Community
"Thanks," *Hill 2000*, May 1971.

The Hill Walk of Fame
The Hill Walk of Fame, (Hill 2000, 2008).

Berra Park
"Circus to Be Here 5 Days in October," *St. Louis Post-Dispatch*, September 20, 1942, p. 19D.
"'Y' Brotherhood Softball Title at Stake Today," *St. Louis Globe-Democrat*, August 25, 1935, p.4C.

Bocce
"England Suffered Their Greatest Ever Humiliation Last Time They Played in a Brazil World
    Cup, Losing 1-0 to USA in 1950," https://www.dailymail.co.uk/sport/worldcup2014/
    article-2644770/England-suffered-GREATEST-EVER-HUMILIATION-time-played-Brazil-
    World-Cup-losing-1-0-USA-1950.html. Accessed April 25, 2020.
Douglas, Geoffrey, *The Game of Their Lives: The Untold Story of the World Cup's Biggest Upset*
    (New York: Harper Collins Publishers Inc., 1996).
The Miracle Match, IFC and Bristol Bay Productions, IFC Films, 2005.

The Great St. Louis Bank Robbery
"Fast Action Foils Bank Robbery," *St. Louis Post-Dispatch*, April 24, 2011, p. M2.
"April 24, 1953: 'This Is a Stickup. Everyone Stand Still.' The Southwest Bank Robbery," *St. Louis
    Post-Dispatch*, April 24, 2020, https://www.stltoday.com/news/local/history/april-24-1953-
    thisis-a-stickup-everyone-stand-still-the-southwest-bank-robbery/article_7398c4be-a4b9-
    50d7-aa73-4afd80fc0549.html. Accessed May 23, 2020.
"I. A. Long, 94; Banker Made World Notice Southwest Bank Rates," *St. Louis Post-Dispatch*,
    November 16, 1993, p. 28.

Prohibition and the Depression
"*The Hill: The Ethnic Heritage of an Urban Neighborhood*, (St. Louis: Social Science Institute,
    Washington University, 1975), pp. 18–23.

Fire Hydrants, Columns, Banners, and Signs
"Neighborhoods of the City of St. Louis," https://www.stlouis-mo.gov/live-work/community/
    neighborhoods/index.cfm. Accessed March 30, 2020.

Hill Day
"Hill Day Promises Entertainment—Culture—Excitement," *Hill 2000*, September 1971, p. 1.

Italian Heritage Parade and Festa
"Columbus Day Parade on Hill," *St. Louis Post-Dispatch*, October 7, 1984, p. 6C.
"Italian Americans Celebrate with Parade," *St. Louis Post-Dispatch*, October 12, 1992, p. 3A.
"Columbus Day Observance," *St. Louis Post-Dispatch*, October 9, 1935, p. 4C.
"Knights to Parade for Columbus Day," *St. Louis Post-Dispatch*, October 11, 1942, p. 19C.

Annual Soap Box Derby and Custom Car Show
St. Louis Soap Box Derby, https://www.soapboxderby.org/st-louis.aspx. Accessed April 15, 2020.
"Going Downhill Fast," *Riverfront Times*, June 5, 2014, https://www.riverfronttimes.com/stlouis/
    goingdownhill-fast/Content?oid=2506218. Accessed April 7, 2020.

Hill House Tour

Ronzio, Judy. "The Hill House Tour: Yesterday, Today and Tomorrow" brochure (Hill Neighborhood Center, June 2018).

Palma Augusta

"Italian American Meeting," *St. Louis Post-Dispatch*, September 20, 1942, p. 19D.

Clubs and Causino

"Joe Causino Memorial Friends of Hill's Youth," *Hill 2000*, May 1971.

"Marguerite Martyn, Uncle Joe Causino, The Gang Buster," *St. Louis Post-Dispatch*, August 30, 1937, p. 3D.

"Severino, Chick. "Hill Clubs Reunion,", *Hill 2000*, November 1985.

Hill 2000

"Use of Mines for Waste Opposed," *St. Louis Post-Dispatch*, March 24, 1970, p. 3.

The Hill: The Ethnic Heritage of an Urban Neighborhood (St. Louis: Social Science Institute, Washington University, 1975), p. 31.

"The Story of Hill 2000," *Hill 2000*, April 1971, p. 1.

Piazza Imo

"Italian Style Piazza Opens in The Hill Neighborhood," *St. Louis Post-Dispatch*, August 19, 2019, p. 1.

"$3 Million Piazza Imo Coming to The Hill," *St. Louis Business Journal*, https://www.bizjournals.com/stlouis/news/2018/06/21/3-million-piazza-imo-coming-to-the-hill.html. Accessed May 6, 2020.

Shaw Community Activity Center

"Shaw School for Swimming Pools," *St. Louis Star and Times*, December 15, 1910, p. 6.

"Wading Pools at Schools Closed as Polio Curb," *St. Louis Star-Times*, July 22, 1949, p. 1.

Maria Russo

"From The Hill to Full Scale Vocal Career," *St. Louis Post-Dispatch,* February 15, 1949.

"Maria Russo on Talent Scouts," *St. Louis Globe-Democrat*, October 1, 1950.

"Thomas Schippers to Be Local Guest Conductor," *St. Louis Globe-Democrat*, November 13, 1955.

Toni Carroll

http://copagirl.com/Pages/AboutToni/AboutToniPage.html. Accessed February 20, 2020.

Gina Galati

https://www.winteroperastl.org/about-us/gina-galati. Accessed February 23, 2020.

Kathryn Favazza

https://www.stlmag.com/events/an-evening-of-opera. Accessed June 16, 2020.

INDEX